Griffin's reliable wisdom and deep belief in the creativity that is rooted inside every one of us. I've dog-eared half the pages of my copy and will be recommending this book to every aspiring and accomplished writer I know!"   —Ellen Bass, author of *Indigo*

"Susan Griffin has given us a guide to the magical music of words and meaning. She walks with us, regaling us with stories and quotes from writers she loves, and shares what she has alchemically distilled over a lifetime of writing, reading and teaching: a precious elixir, as if gently pressed from thousands of roses."
—Deirdre English, former editor of *Mother Jones* magazine and lecturer at UC Berkeley Graduate School of Journalism

"With her signature gifts of insight, skill, and subtlety, Susan Griffin simultaneously demystifies and elevates the art of creative writing. Relevant across all genres and levels of experience, this book is so practical and elegant, so intelligent and essential—I can't wait to share it with every writer I know."
—Elizabeth Rosner, author of *Survivor Café: The Legacy of Trauma and the Labyrinth of Memory*

"*Out of Silence, Sound. Out of Nothing, Something.* is a gorgeous, uncanny book that goes to the heart of why and how we write. It is, yes, a guide, but like all of Susan Griffin's work, it turns on the wisdom and sensibility of a philosopher poet. I'll recommend it to every writer I know, every student I teach, anyone who leans across a table and whispers, 'What I really want to do is write.'"
—Honor Moore, author of *Our Revolution: A Mother and Daughter at Midcentury*

"Beautifully organized, lucidly written, Susan Griffin's *Out of Silence, Sound. Out of Nothing, Something,* is destined to become an inspiring guide for creative writing classes and for creative writers on their own, at the laptop or in the library."

—Sandra M. Gilbert, coauthor of *Still Mad* and
The Madwoman in the Attic

"Susan Griffin shares her many insights into the phenomenon of writing with a clarity and feeling that can open doors to the new writer or deepen the experience for those already writing. A must read-for anyone about to take pen in hand, or put hand to keyboard."
—Leonard Pitt, author and theater artist

Out of Silence, **Sound.**
Out of Nothing, **Something.**

Out of Silence, Sound.

Out of Nothing, Something.

A Writer's Guide

Susan Griffin

Counterpoint
BERKELEY, CALIFORNIA

Out of Silence, Sound.
Out of Nothing, Something.

First Counterpoint edition: 2023

Library of Congress Cataloging-in-Publication Data
Names: Griffin, Susan, author.
Title: Out of silence, sound. Out of nothing, something : a writer's guide /
    Susan Griffin.
Description: First Counterpoint edition. | Berkeley, California : Counterpoint,
    2023.
Identifiers: LCCN 2022023050 | ISBN 9781640094109 (trade paperback) |
    ISBN 9781640094116 (ebook)
Subjects: LCSH: Authorship—Technique. | Creative writing.
Classification: LCC PN145 .G75 2023 | DDC 808.02—dc23/eng/20220727
LC record available at https://lccn.loc.gov/2022023050

Cover design and illustration by Dana Li
Book design by Laura Berry

COUNTERPOINT
2560 Ninth Street, Suite 318
Berkeley, CA 94710
www.counterpointpress.com

Printed in the United States of America

10 9 8 7 6 5 4 3 2

*In memory of my adoptive parents, educator and artist
Geraldine and Morton Dimondstein,
who gave me more than I can ever say.*

Contents

Out of Silence, **Sound.**
Out of Nothing, **Something.**

Introduction

Make It Your Own

If there is a basic premise that lies underneath *Out of Silence, Sound. Out of Nothing, Something*, it is the notion that human beings are all creative. I am not alone in the belief that creativity is a birthright belonging to us all. And it's not only human beings who are innately creative. We live in a creative universe.

Think of it: conception, birth, mutation, transformation occur so frequently all around us that we often take creation for granted. As over millennia young squirrels or blue jays or rose buds or plum blossoms appear each spring, as new species of beetles or turtles or viruses materialize, as a lush green landscape gradually morphs into a spare brown expanse before our eyes, or clouds appear to render rain or slowly dissolve, turning red as the sun goes down, everything we see participates in an endless round of change that is ultimately, in all its manifestations, including evolution and climate change, creative.

Yet no matter how frequent and familiar this phenomenon may be, it has often been said that creativity, especially creative writing, cannot really be taught. I do not agree. It is true, though, that besides a variety of wonderful books on how to write, there are also ineffective approaches, ways of teaching often adopted by those who, while admiring literature, do not write themselves. Lacking any direct experience, such well-meaning instructors rely too often on a thicket of methods more appropriate to the corporate world or military training than to generating literature.

This book is meant to guide readers through the process of writing. It takes a kind and gentle approach, one which I have adopted over five decades of teaching writers and those who wish to write. Based on an abiding faith in human ingenuity, each chapter is meant to help the reader through the many stages required to create a work of literature, be it fiction or nonfiction, prose or poetry.

The chapters are short; the space between them indicates the time needed to absorb each teaching, and meditate on it. These chapters are arranged according to an imagined but not always followed (or even appropriate) chronology of the process of writing, from beginning to end. Part I, "Before the Beginning," addresses and encourages the elusive process through which ideas, images, plots, or stray words develop, which precedes any creative work. Part II, "Writing," contains various lessons on how to write, knowledge I have gained from writing several books and, perhaps more relevant, from my students, while guiding several generations. Finally, Part III, "The Means to an End," aims to help the writer find an ending that is good and right.

You can read this book from beginning to end as you would any other book, or you can dip into it as you wish or need. Because just like writing, reading is also a creative experience. Make it your own.

Heaven and earth begin in the unnamed: name's the mother of the ten thousand things.

—LAO TZU, *The Tao Te Ching*
(TRANS. URSULA K. LE GUIN)

PART I

Before the Beginning

Silence

Consider this: at one time, all the stories we know so well, every line we may have memorized from a poem or a play, all the literature that has shaped our collective imagination, did not exist. Whether it be that powerful first line, "No man is an island," from a poem by John Donne, or the ghost story that drives Toni Morrison's novel *Beloved*, or Thomas Jefferson's famous phrase from the Declaration of Independence, "We hold these truths to be self-evident," there was a time when all these words that are so familiar to us had not yet been written. Where today there is the sound of words, once there was silence.

Mystery

There is an inexpressible magic by which something comes from nothing, a miracle of creation that happens all over the world not just once, but again and again. As frequently as this conjuring act occurs, it never seems commonplace.

This is not a predictable process. To produce anything of value, you must travel over a narrow bridge between resolve and acceptance. Whether it's a few words, an image, a turn in the plot, the manner in which the narrator speaks, you cannot control exactly what will come to you. After all, if you knew exactly what was coming, it would not be new. But you can prepare the ground.

(How I Learned to Write)

It didn't happen suddenly or even overnight. As I remember it, I made my first attempts at writing when I was about ten years old. I was by myself in the back bedroom of my grandparents' home, the room with peach-colored walls that had been designated as mine. A single bed where I slept was placed against the wall facing my grandmother's sewing machine, which was placed against the opposite wall. There was a chair she used while sewing, but I never sat in it. I preferred sitting on the floor when I wrote, or attempted to write (or thought about writing), laboriously printing words in a thick, narrow, rectangular pad filled with newsprint that made ink bleed. My stated intention—what I told everyone I was doing—was to write a novel.

I certainly had enough material. My immediate family had been torn apart almost violently by my mother's persistent alcoholism. She had an affair with a man in our neighborhood, though her drinking preceded that dalliance by many years. When my parents divorced we all went our separate ways, my sister to my great-aunt's house six hundred miles north, my father to a shabby bachelor's apartment in North Hollywood, my mother to a small room in the San Fernando Valley, me to my mother's parents in Los Angeles.

It was a dramatic story, filled with pain and loss. But at ten years of age in 1953, it never occurred to me to tell it. From the heavy silences within and outside my family, I sensed my parents' divorce and my mother's alcoholism were shameful. In any case, I was aiming for something more heroic. Novels, I gathered from what was popular at the time (think of *The Naked and the Dead*, or *From Here to Eternity*), had to be about combat and soldiers of some kind. So, that was the subject I chose. There would be a soldier involved and a woman who loved him waiting for his return.

The problem was of course that, except for loss, I knew hardly anything at all about war. Nor did I have any idea about how to conduct research. However, the main problem was that, beyond my ambition, I had no inner connection to the subject. So, no wonder the writing came out in tiny spurts before the well ran entirely dry.

I was, however, learning.

Paying Attention

I cannot summon up inspiration; I myself am summoned.
—P. L. TRAVERS, AUTHOR OF *Mary Poppins*

The idea of a blank page can be daunting, frightening enough to stop you in your tracks. But, fortunately, the blank page is not really where most writers begin. With a few exceptions, that page usually appears much further along in the process, when you are better prepared to meet the challenge.

Most often, whether fiction or nonfiction, a play or an essay, a work of literature makes its first appearance in a far less developed form—febrile, subtle, hardly articulated, not yet delineated in any way. To find the beginning of something in this embryonic state, you will need to pay attention to the thoughts that pass through your own mind, or to put it another way, you will need to learn to pay attention to your own attention. Where are your thoughts drifting? What seems to draw your interest over and over? What subject will make you rush to see a film or read a book that has just been released? What idea or place, person or event, whenever mentioned or alluded to, quickens you, making your heart beat a little faster, filling you with energy?

The process often feels as if you are being called to discover an unknown territory, full of hidden meanings that seem to lie in wait, meanings that can seem almost palpable yet just out of reach, whether hidden inside the subject that draws your interest or inside yourself.

It may begin inauspiciously. A neighbor's front porch light is always on at night, for instance, and two nights in a row, at three in the morning, you see a young man sitting on the steps. After a while, you find this observation turning into a story. Or perhaps you just have a hunch, an outlier notion, about a current minor political issue, in which no one else seems to be as interested as you are and to which, nevertheless, despite all your attempts to abandon this idea, your attention keeps returning. Bit by bit you find yourself formulating an argument. Then again it may start with a compelling dream. Or even with what seems like a fleeting observation, except that it stays in your mind, like the grain of sand that irritates an oyster (and let's hope this results in a pearl). Or it might be a story you heard as a child and only dimly remembered until one day this tale suddenly comes to the surface, carrying with it a host of new insights. Or is it a story you come across when you are looking for something else? Yet again, perhaps you are obsessed with a celebrity, a film, a novel, a painting. (More than one book or film or story or poem has been inspired by previous works such as Jane Austen's *Pride and Prejudice* or Billy Wilder's *Sunset Boulevard*.) But perhaps it is not just a memory that moves you but instead a sensation, the taste, for instance, of a particular cookie, called a madeleine, dipped into a cup of tea.

And once I had recognized the taste of the crumb of madeleine soaked in her decoction of lime-flowers which my aunt used to give me (although I did not yet know and must long postpone the discovery of why this memory made me so happy) immediately the old grey house upon the street, where her room was, rose up like the scenery of a theatre to attach itself to the little pavilion, opening on to the garden, which had been built out behind it for my parents (the isolated panel which until that moment had been all that I could see); and with the house the town, from morning to night and in all weathers, the Square where I was sent before luncheon, the streets along which I used to run errands, the country roads we took when it was fine.

—MARCEL PROUST, *Swann's Way, Volume 1,*
In Search of Lost Time

Focus

Focus. The effect can feel like magic. While paying attention to your own attention intensifies your gaze, you notice that references to your subject, whatever that is, seem to multiply around you. If you have set your novel in Norway, for instance, a magazine to which you subscribe has devoted several pages to traveling up the fjords, and soon after, you hear from close friends that they are planning a trip there. A day later as you are listening to the radio, you find that the man being interviewed was once an ambassador to Norway. Is this simply coincidence, or something that always happens, yet you failed to notice before?

Whatever the cause, welcome the deluge, if for no other reason than as a sign that you are on the right path.

Of course, synchronicity cannot and should not replace the research that so often is required for what you write.

Still just as you would do as you conduct any kind of research, take notes on what you notice, hear, see, whether stories or single words, intuitions or ideas (or the subtle inclinations that the French writer Nathalie Sarraute famously called *tropisms*). You never know what will end up being significant or useful.

Index cards are especially helpful for this purpose because as the work develops subcategories, your notes, if they are on separate cards, can be arranged in different ways, by chapters or according to various categories. And while organizing your notes this way, you will also be building the structure of the work you are writing, without solidifying it yet into an outline. (Outlines are very useful, but when they are constructed too early in the process, they can constrict your creativity.)

Tropismes was the title of the first book written by Nathalie Sarraute, one of France's most celebrated writers. At the time it was published, *Tropismes* was considered an experimental work. Eschewing the sturdy, often voluminous plots that characterized novels by Zola, Hugo, and Balzac, as with Virginia Woolf and James Joyce, she was more interested in capturing the inner life than the action featured in classical narratives. Like a plant leaning toward the light, *Tropismes* follows her inclinations, as she writes about whatever memories, incidents, or scenes come to mind, trusting that within this collage new meanings will be made clear.

Common Knowledge

We have all inherited an endless supply of advice woven into the culture we share, a gift of wisdom, craft, techniques, manners, expectations, and, of course, ways of seeing. Most of us would find it hard to survive without this repository of knowledge gathered over millennia. Yet very often, a creative work departs from what is called common knowledge. Take *Pride and Prejudice*, for example. In Elizabeth Bennet, Austen has created one of the most memorable characters in literature. Her appeal comes, not in small part, from the ways she strays from the conventions prescribed for women in nineteenth-century England. She does not defer to those who enjoy a higher position in society than she does. She often speaks her mind, even when she expresses herself through irony. Indeed, in the period when the novel was written, what scholar Claudia Johnson calls her "outrageous unconventionality" was "very daring." And the daring did not belong to Elizabeth alone. In order to bring her to life, Jane Austen had to be daring first.

Bucking the tide can be a heady thrill. Yet in the end, not only naughty children but adults too face consequences. You don't want to be unruly just for the sake of it. The key to knowing whether or not you should depart from common knowledge lies within both the work you are doing and the vision within you that drives the work. Ask yourself what the core of that vision is.

Once you locate that core, whenever you bring it to mind, it will give you the courage you need to break with convention. Courage, as no doubt you've been told before, betrays its nature in the syllable *cour*, a derivative of the French *coeur* meaning "heart." If the heart of the work requires you to color outside the lines, then you must do so. And by the way (more on this later) the heart of the work must be connected, in some way, to *your* heart. Meaning, quite simply, the book moves you (in the same way that it will eventually move your readers).

Reading

If you want to take up writing, it's imperative that you read literature of all kinds. Even when you choose to depart from literary conventions, you will need to know not only what they are but how to incorporate them into the library of forms that you carry around in your mind. As much as a departure departs, it is also connected to the past, to the point of departure and the roads leading there. But much more important than a critical apprehension of this literary inheritance is to have a physical sense, an experience of the sounds, the shapes, the almost palpable odor of attitudes and postures, the weight of grammar and vocabulary, all of which belong to the traditions that have preceded and, in fact, shaped you.

Taking Time

In the late nineteenth and early twentieth centuries, industrial engineers developed a model that dictated what motions were most efficient and how much time each task should take. Though labor unions objected to the wide application of this method, we still live in a world that places tangible profits and thus measurable production above every other value. Accordingly, we are tempted to weigh the worth of what we do in numbers: the number of hours we have spent at a desk, the number of words we have produced, the number of pages, and, eventually, the number of books sold.

But unless you are on a daily press deadline, this is not by any means the best atmosphere for creative work. For one thing, many of your most fruitful insights occur when you are away from your desk. When confronted with a problem you don't seem to be able to solve, for instance, often the best course is to walk away. Quite literally. Walk into the next room and stare out the window, refresh your coffee. Take a walk around the block. Don't force it. Just return your focus lightly to your subject from time to time. Then watch the magic happen.

Your solution may not appear immediately or even on the same day that you seek it. When you plant a seed in the ground, there is a natural rhythm according to which the seed will sprout and grow into the flower, the head of lettuce, or the carrot you want. You must be respectful of this timing. Creative efforts require the same patience. If you let the work evolve within you at a natural pace, you will often be surprised by what emerges. Even when you are writing a memoir or describing an event from history for which you believe you have all the facts you need, as you write, you will discover new elements and perspectives that transform your own ideas about the subject you have chosen.

Even subtle details can set a new direction in motion. If you decide to make the fictional character you are creating severely myopic, for instance, you might treat this as a metaphor, as if this character is shortsighted. On the other hand, this may not be how you see this character at all, even if, at the same time, his or her myopia has begun to seem essential to your story. The solution may not occur to you immediately. Yet after a few hours, a day, a week, or even longer, you begin to sense that this character sees more deeply than many others who have 20/20 vision. If you take the time to follow the winding, unpredictable paths creative work demands, you will be moving, as the great Grace Paley once said, "from what you know into what you don't know."

Wings

In *Zorba the Greek*, the novel by Nikos Kazantzakis, the narrator tells the following story. One morning he finds a cocoon in a tree where he sees that a butterfly is making a hole, getting ready to come out. He waits, but since it is taking so long to appear, he grows impatient. Finally, he bends over it, breathing on it to warm it. And as he does this, a "miracle begins to happen" before his eyes. The cocoon begins to open and the butterfly starts slowly crawling out. But he tells us, "I shall never forget my horror when I saw how its wings were folded back and crumpled; the wretched butterfly tried with its whole trembling body to unfold them." His breath had forced the butterfly to appear before its time. "It struggled desperately and, a few seconds later, died in the palm of my hand."

"I realize today," he tells us, "that it is a mortal sin to violate the great laws of nature. We should not hurry, we should not be impatient, but we should confidently obey the external rhythm."

Reverie

What other psychological freedom do we have
than the freedom to dream?

—GASTON BACHELARD,
The Poetics of Reverie

It used to be, and probably still is in many classrooms, a common practice to chastise and humiliate any student who is caught looking out the window, fixed in a rapt gaze at seemingly nothing at all. But with all due sympathy to any teacher who wishes her or his lessons to be heard, such moments of reverie are known to yield many creative insights.

In his journal, Emerson tells us that one Sunday, when he was in church and supposed to be listening to a sermon, he found himself inexorably drawn to the landscape he could see just outside the window. He could not take his eyes off the snow that was steadily falling. This was much more interesting, he wrote, than the preacher's words that morning. In more ways than one, his attention was drifting from the doctrine of the church to the teachings of nature.

According to her close friend, the novelist Mary McCarthy, the great political philosopher Hannah Arendt was known to spend hours at a window or simply staring into space while she allowed her thoughts to wander.

Reverie is a natural state of mind that can only occur when the mind is at rest, not fixated on any particular task, but empty, if not of content, of any restraint or obligation. Close to sleep but not sleep, the waking dream, or reverie, allows the dreamer to pass boundaries and in the process discover new insights or (as Freud well understood) forgotten memories.

Whether you have discovered an enchanted world, or what may seem like a trash bin of the heart and mind, it is from this land of semiconscious thoughts that some of the best literature emerges.

Faithful

> Of this there can be no question—creative work requires a loyalty as complete as the loyalty of water to the force of gravity.
>
> —MARY OLIVER

I doubt that any of Picasso's many lovers would characterize him as faithful. But he was unwaveringly faithful to his work. He showed up unfailingly day after day to stand before an easel or bend over a sketch pad. One artist after another gives the same advice to beginners. "Show up," as Isabel Allende says. Or as Tchaikovsky warned, "A self-respecting artist must not fold his (or her) hands on the pretext that he is not in the mood."

Above all what you need to do is be there, alone in your study or at your desk, ready. This requires that you appoint a time. Write it in your schedule. And if anyone asks if you are free at that hour, you can say you have an appointment.

You might eventually discard anything you write. You may produce only a sentence or two. Or nothing at all. What is important is that you are present to the process. Being there, while focusing on nothing else, will ignite your creative mind. The results may not appear immediately. Yet somehow out of sight, your mind will be working. The delay resembles those times when you are asked a question for which you cannot think of an answer until hours later, when the perfect response comes to you. If you keep showing up, eventually what you are seeking will show up too.

Seed

With many beginning writers, or even those who have written several books, it helps to start with small periods of time. This way you are not overwhelmed. Anyone can carve out fifteen minutes of silent solitude during which you may write nothing, but nevertheless you keep a soft focus on your subject. The effect of this is like watering a seed. Though you can't see it in the beginning, in response to the attention you give it, the plant is laying down roots and growing, until one day it emerges, a surprise, yet one that indeed you have cultivated. Fed by brief but regular visits to your subject, just below ordinary consciousness, your mind is indeed working long hours, creating a work of literature.

False Starts

Don't be afraid of false starts. Literature is like science in this way. Negative results are useful. If you are uncomfortable with what you have written, ask yourself why. Answering this question is as creative as anything else you will do as an artist. Though sometimes you will not be able to give a direct, logical answer. Rather, you might find the answer through trial and error. Try a different tone, for instance. The tone that is right will *feel* right to you. As I wrote a book about the women known as courtesans, I began one version with lush poetic lines. But after a half page I could not continue. The sound of the words I had written felt wrong. Eventually I settled on a slightly ironic professor's voice, worldly and sophisticated. Only later did I realize this voice more accurately reflected my subjects, who were cultivated, savvy, and shrewd. The right tone or voice will lend you the energy you need to move ahead. The same is true for all your stylistic choices. It could be for instance that you are not using the verb tense that is best for your work. You've written "she had an idea," yet now that seems somehow wrong to you. But when you change it slightly to "she has an idea," the sentence suddenly feels right. Shifting to the present tense may seem minor, but a small alteration can create a seismic shift in the tone of your book and even your own mood as you write. In the case of writing about courtesans, the slightly ironic tone I adopted allowed me to see the larger picture, one that involved society, gender, and of course commerce. But before I could find the irony in my subject matter, I had to listen inwardly to my own negative response to what had been a false start.

Your Mood

As long as you are paying attention to your thoughts, be aware of your own mood too. Do you feel like Lillian Hellman, as she was portrayed in the film *Julia*, when, in exasperation, she threw her typewriter out the window? Then again, your own writing may be putting you to sleep. Whatever you are feeling as you write— whether you are bored, exhilarated, rapturous, solemn, studious, fascinated, angry, sad—will somehow make its way onto the page, and as a result the reader will feel what you are feeling as you write. Take time to find the words and images or ideas that please and excite you in some way. Don't settle for less.

Start Where You Are

This is the title of a book by the great meditation teacher Pema Chödrön. "You can feel like the world's most hopeless basket case, but that feeling is your wealth," she writes. She wrote this as part of a guide to what she has called "compassionate living." But this is also what writers need to hear. As you write, you will find great wealth in all the sides of yourself, emotions, memories, stories that embarrass or, even worse, shame you. If you let go of what you think you should say and ought to be or do, and accept who and what you really are (saying or doing), you have found the best starting point.

In the days before I began to write my book *Woman and Nature*, while I was washing dishes, I found myself listening to a radio broadcast about the dangers of plutonium. What I heard about this highly toxic substance disturbed me profoundly. Would I ever be able to protect my six-year-old daughter from this danger? *I should include this in the book I'm going to write*, I thought. But then my heart sank. *How can I write about this? I know so little. Even if I learn more about it, no one will really care about my opinion; I am not a scientist.*

For several moments I felt powerless. But then, after a few more moments of despair, I realized that this feeling was exactly what I had to contribute. I wrote a long paragraph expressing the sense of utter powerlessness that ordinary people feel when faced with this threat.

When Tony Judt wrote the chapter called "Food" in his memoir, *The Memory Chalet*, was he tempted to leave out any mention of his love for the less than fashionable food he ate as a child? Yet this particular taste, which a lesser writer might have wanted to hide, gave him a wonderful first sentence. "Just because you grow up on bad food, it does not follow that you lack nostalgia for it." The line wins us over immediately, not only through curiosity, but because magically it has made us coconspirators in his deviation from the dictates of good taste.

We hear there is a substance and it is called plutonium. We hear that "they" are somewhere (do you remember the name of the state?) manufacturing it. We don't know how it is made. We think the substance uranium is used. We know it is radioactive. We have seen the photographs of babies and children deformed from radiation. The substance plutonium becomes interesting to us when we read that certain parts of buildings where it is manufactured have leaks. We don't know really what this means, if it is like the leak in our roofs or the water pipe in the back yard, or if it is a simple word for a process beyond our comprehension. But we know the word "leak" indicates error and we know that there is no room for error in the handling of this substance. That it has been called the most deadly substance known. That the smallest particle (can one see a particle, smell it?) can cause cancer if breathed, if ingested. All that we know in the business of living eludes us in this instant.

—SUSAN GRIFFIN, *Woman and Nature*

More About Voice

In any given work, no matter the genre or subject matter, not only is the right voice critical, you really cannot start until you have found it. The voice you use is not external to the content of what you are writing. It's as integral to the work as you are.

John Berger has written a marvelous description of the voice within a series of signs he encountered, posted in the building where he used to swim, admonishing visitors for instance that THE HAIR DRYER WILL BE SHUT OFF 5 MINUTES BE-FORE CLOSING TIME or warning that THE ENTRY THROUGH THIS DOOR IS FORBIDDEN TO ANY PERSON WHO IS NOT A MEMBER OF STAFF, THANK YOU. He calls this "a measured, impersonal committee voice—with somewhere in the distance a child laughing."

Coming from the opposite direction, Michael Ondaatje's memoir, *Running in the Family*, begins with a line that is intensely personal. "What began it all was the bright bone of dream I could hardly hold onto," he writes, immediately establishing an intimate and trusting relationship with you, the reader, as if you were in the middle of a conversation.

Voice is not the same as point of view. While having an indelible effect on everything you write, voice is far more intimate with your unconscious mind. Defining "voice" is not easy. It is a living mélange of style, psychology, posture, opinion, background, and culture that conveys all these elements through sound.

In some works, as with for instance Eudora Welty's short story, "Why I Live at the P.O.," the voice, in this case the voice of the narrator who is also a character, is unreliable (and yet in this story, also irresistible). In a book like Eileen Myles's autobiography,

Inferno, the voice—irreverent, rebellious, lazily defying "good taste"—is often more compelling than the story. Both of these books are narrated in the first person, by an "I." But voice can be felt through a "you," a "we," or even a supposedly omniscient, unengaged narrator too.

The voice of a novel by Henry James or Edith Wharton, written in the third person, with an omniscient and therefore almost invisible narrator, conveys a quiet authority, the implied expertise of a man or a woman raised in an upper-class household and educated in the "best schools," whose grammar is impeccable, and who, though not nearly as dry as a well-behaved school teacher, seems well informed, almost authoritative, and politely confident, even when conveying wit, sorrow, or a devastating insight.

Most often you do not choose your voice, at least not immediately. More frequently, your voice will choose you. That is, you hear it (in your head of course). Or you may stumble across it whether in a book, an article, a newspaper story, a character's speech in an old movie. Maybe it's Clint Eastwood's gruff voice that suddenly seems to open doors in your mind. Or you may encounter it in a poem by Lucille Clifton:

> me and you be sisters.
> we be the same.

This is not Clifton's ordinary grammar or voice. But it's one with which she was familiar. A voice *she* heard, a grammar she knew well.

If you find the right voice it will act as a kind of catalyst, helping your words to flow, producing results often far better than you imagined.

A Brief Word About Grammars

Determining what is and is not grammatically correct is more complex than most of us were taught in grade school. This is because languages often have several different grammars reflecting the different versions of a given language spoken by diverse groups. British English is not the same as American English. In the United States, for instance, English spoken in Los Angeles differs from English spoken in the Bronx or New Orleans. And in the United Kingdom a different form of English is spoken in Manchester, not to speak of Ireland, Scotland, and Wales, than in London. And within London, you will encounter a number of different versions of English, often, as with Cockney, determined by class. Cockney is not incorrect. It is simply different. It is, however, possible to speak any of these versions of English incorrectly because each has its own grammar.

Grammar is not simply a set of rules. It's a system of thought, and you can use it to think more clearly. Among other valuable bits of information, it will tell you who did what to whom (subject, verb, and object or indirect object), and when, whether now, in the past, the distant past, or the future.

Moreover, correct grammar constitutes an agreement between those who speak any language, a contract that ensures the patterns of words in a sentence will make sense to those who are listening (or reading).

Outlines

To know what you're going to draw, you have to begin
drawing . . . What I capture in spite of myself interests me
more than my own ideas.   —PABLO PICASSO

Professors and publishers are prone to demand outlines from writers. That sounds like a reasonable request. After all, if you are working with an architect or contractor you'll want to see the plans. The
problem is if you try to create a linear outline of a potential work
too quickly, more often than not, you'll be killing the goose that
lays the golden eggs.

At the same time, as you gather notes, dreams, observations,
and references, you may be sensing connections. More likely than
not, these connections have not taken a linear form yet, and when
you attempt to force linear logic on them, you may sense that they
tend to lose their vitality.

But a graphic representation of the connections you have noted
does not have to be linear, and it can reveal connections you had
not seen before. Instead of a progression from A to Z, you can draw
a spiderlike web, with both horizontal and vertical lines connecting subjects and ideas, a scheme that allows some subjects to have
more than one, perhaps even several, connections. What results
often resembles the root system of a plant or the circulatory system
of animals. In other words it mimics living anatomies in nature,
which are themselves both communicative and creative.

As you continue writing, any outline, including one that is not
linear, can and probably will change. Over time, of course, as the
work evolves and a consecutive order begins to appear, you will be
able to create outlines that are more linear.

A Desk

There have been and still are lots of writers who write in transit. But many writers, myself included, feel the need for a stable place to write, a reliable desk to which you can return day after day. A place where you keep the pens you like, the computer you use most often, books to which you may refer, hard copy drafts, notes—in short, all you will need in the course of a day's work. Though it's not just the fact that this desk holds the equipment you need. Another factor comes into play, one that is hard to explain or even pin down. This is that a stable desk seems to emanate a kind of spiritual gravity, pulling you, instead of toward the earth, into whatever book or poem or play, reportage or opinion piece you are working on. Is this a mystical process or a phenomenon easily explained by psychology and cognitive science? Or is it a combination of both? I cannot say. I only know it is real and that is why I recommend, if possible, setting up a desk devoted to your work and no other task, whether chopping onions or solving jigsaw puzzles.

A Room of Her (His or Their) Own

A woman must have money if she is to write . . .
—VIRGINIA WOOLF, *A Room of One's Own*

Actually, Woolf said, "if she is to write fiction." But the wisdom applies to other genres as well. A man, of course, will need money too. However, in general, such support is still more available for him than it is for women, unless the writer of any gender is part of another marginalized community. Regarding which, Alice Walker writes in *The Same River Twice*, "as people of color and as women, as non-establishment or politically disempowered people, we face an increasing challenge simply to stay alive on the planet."

This precarity extends to the conditions a writer needs in order to write, an art that requires time and space, the former provided by grants from foundations or advances from publishers (because writers too must pay rent and buy groceries,) the latter provided by a room or at least a quiet corner of a quiet room. And once, despite unfavorable circumstances, a literary work is actually completed, the precarity does not stop, but instead continues in the form of hostile reviews or no notice at all.

To meet these formidable challenges the marginalized writer must call on a sense of inner authority. This can be difficult to achieve if you have been the object of prejudice, especially since, as playwright Wajahat Ali has said,* so often you internalize these attacks and thus are tempted to silence your own voice. To prevent this destructive process, you will have to build a conceptual room,

---

*In conversation with Dave Eggers, San Francisco City Arts and Lectures

a safe house in your mind where your ideas, your imagination, and finally your words are valued.

Of course, this is necessary for all writers, marginalized or not. If you do not have an inner authority, readers will be less willing to read past the first page. Whatever their response to what you write, they must be able to trust you. And to win their trust, you have to trust yourself.

. . . Shakespeare had a sister . . . She died young—
alas she never wrote a word. She lies buried where
the omnibuses now stop, opposite the Elephant
and the Castle. Now my belief is that this poet
who never wrote a word and was buried at the
crossroads still lives. She lives in you and in me,
and in many other women who are not here to-
night, for they are washing up the dishes and putting the children to bed.

—VIRGINIA WOOLF, *A Room of One's Own*

Killing the Angel in the House

While you are writing or thinking about writing, you do not want to hear what others nearby are saying, or feel obliged to answer their questions and requests, or even consider their needs.

This is an especially pressing issue for women who, more often than not, will be visited by what Virginia Woolf calls (using a phrase popular at the time) "the angel in the house." From time to time, this angel lands on a woman's shoulder to whisper to her that she ought to be offering someone else in the household a warm cup of coffee or that the words the writer is using to describe someone or something seem too harsh. Woolf's advice, if ruthless, is still correct. Kill the angel.

Silenced

There are many kinds of silence in the life of a writer. One is the quiet of a soundscape that surrounds you, as if the air were listening, eager to hear your words. Another is the silence that is imposed on a writer who does not have or is not given the time to write. And there is another silence, the consequence of censorship of all kinds, through which either directly or indirectly a writer is told that the story on the tip of her or his tongue must not be told. Perhaps the command to remain silent has come from a brutal dictator like Joseph Stalin (who sent more than one writer to Siberia) or from a tyrannous government official like Joseph McCarthy (who condemned a number of screenwriters in Hollywood to silence), or perhaps the censorship has come from a more intimate source. You might want to tell a secret story about your family or perhaps reveal a crime, to write about the way you were sexually or emotionally abused as a child, or perhaps you simply want to write about your last love affair without hurting anyone's feelings.

The problem is that not telling a story you want to tell will often stop you from writing anything. It is like that undigested food that has made you lose your appetite. It may seem like advice that is too simple, but what I suggest is that you tell the story in any case, with an unwritten agreement with yourself that you will not publish it or perhaps not even show it to anyone. At the very least this will allow you to move on to other stories. And by one of those inexplicable miracles that sometimes occur in the process of writing, by telling the very story you were told not to tell, you may experience an inner sea change that allows you finally to share it with the world. For which the world will be grateful, since when they are revealed, very often, secrets make very good stories indeed.

Form

Forms are everywhere. Two of the many trees I can see outside my window share a form. They are both Monterey pines, tall, with long branches and perennially green needles, some of which they shed in all seasons. As you walk over these needles, each step yields a scent I associate with the summer camp where I spent many summers as a child. The form that shapes them is in the DNA they inherited, a form that inhabits my mind too, forever associated with a series of vividly personal memories.

Literature itself *is* a form. A form that can hold memories, associations, judgments, fantasies, dreams, prayers, information, knowledge of all kinds, and even mysteries, which is to say, even what we don't know. As with DNA, we inherit the form of literature, along with all the forms within this form. Like a set of Russian dolls, within the category of literature, one finds poetry, and within that several other forms, epic, free verse, villanelles, or sonnets, and within each of those, such as the sonnet, several other forms, for instance, the Petrarchan sonnet (invented by Petrarch), or the curtal sonnet (used by Gerard Manley Hopkins). The paradox of form, which mirrors the paradox haunting all traditions, is that, as with DNA, forms tend to give birth to variations.

Forms are not at all passive. They have a powerful effect not just on the final version, but on the process of creation itself. They can and will guide you both consciously and unconsciously in particular directions. And though we talk about form as opposed to content, they cannot really be separated. Form is more than just a pretty wrapping. Steadily but surely, it not only shapes but merges with content.

Once, while I was teaching a writing class to a group of beginning students, I invited them to taste carrots prepared in two different ways. The only difference lay in how they were sliced, one portion grated, the other sliced in rounds. The students were amazed to find out how different they tasted. (Grated carrots are much sweeter.)

The ways you shape your subject will create distinct experiences and, in this way, express different meanings.

Take the sonnet for example. The formula for a classic sonnet, though it has many variations, is as follows: three quatrains (four lines each) with alternating rhyme and, at the end, a couplet, which contains what is called a volta, a turn in an unexpected direction. The term came from the Italian word for "little song," *sonetto*, which started out as a love song, a history that infuses every sonnet, whether it is a declaration of love or not. John Wyatt brought it to England in the sixteenth century (where it was practiced famously by Shakespeare).

Still carrying this history within its rules, this form is alive and well in contemporary literature. "The Tradition," a stunning sonnet by Jericho Brown, after naming flowers, begins by invoking the cosmos and ends in a powerful turn, or volta, with the four lines below.

> Too late, sped the video to see blossoms
> Brought in seconds, colors you expect in poems
> Where the world ends, everything cut down.
> John Crawford. Eric Garner. Mike Brown.

This is a different kind of love poem. The rhyme between "cut down" and "Mike Brown" is heart-wrenching. With its steady reassuring rhythm and rhyme, the sonnet prepares the reader to be shocked by these deaths, and gives us, without saying it, a visceral understanding that such murders threaten the order of the cosmos we all share.

The Right One

What is the right form for what you plan to write?

This is a question that only you can answer.

What you need to find is the form that best serves what you will write. Sometimes the idea for a work comes already attached to a form. Sometimes you are drawn to the form and it's a subject you need to find. But if you have a subject without a form, a good way to find what will work well is trial and error. The right form will allow your ideas and words to flow more easily.

New and Old

We live in an age that values innovation more than tradition. After the massacres that occurred on the battlefields of World War I, a general disillusion descended, one that affected the arts as well as politics. The creative explosion that had begun before the war, at the turn of the century, accelerated, with startling new images in canvases by Picasso, Braque, and Miró and remarkable departures in literature from Gertrude Stein to André Breton to Ernest Hemingway. Our love affair with innovation has continued into the twenty-first century, even in the tools we use to create images and record words, from computers, to apps, to social media.

It is predictable though that in the midst of all this modernity, another trend should appear, the revival of old forms, canvases that resemble the precision achieved by the old masters, essays with the quiet dignified tone of Montaigne, epic poems. And, in truth, innovative forms do not depart from tradition entirely. Instead, they introduce variations and new applications of ancient habits.

Whether early Native American poetry or the *Iliad* or eighth-century poetry from the Tang Dynasty by Li Po, ancient forms contain wisdom beyond the content they hold.

Take the use of repetition in poetry. It's an age-old technique, one that mimics the repetitions, or patterns, found throughout nature, including the symmetry of the human body. As in, we have two ears—two ears that taken together are able to receive sound from more than one direction. (And in this sense, the repetition in the human body echoes the multidirectional nature of sound.)

Considering stories, we are so habituated to telling them, we don't think about narration as a form. But it is one of the oldest we have inherited, coming to us from a time before writing, when literature was oral, passed from one generation of storytellers to the next. Storytelling helps us all to think about cause and effect, the consequences of what we do, as well as acknowledging a larger context, the human and natural conditions that have preceded and surround us now, including the larger realms in which we do not have control over what happens next in the plot.

Night Chant
(A Navajo healing prayer)

Tségihi,
House made of dawn.
House made of evening light.
House made of the dark cloud.
House made of male rain.
House made of dark mist.
House made of female rain.
House made of pollen.
House made of grasshoppers.
Dark cloud is at the door.
The trail out of it is dark cloud.

(How I Learned to Write)

Soon after my failed attempt at a war novel, I began to read passages out loud from books I liked. I had listened many times to my older sister, who was studying drama in high school, as she read passages from plays or poems out loud. So, as with practically everything she did, I followed her example. To whomever would listen, I read stories by Hans Christian Andersen, Edna St. Vincent Millay's stirring poem, "Renascence," dialogues from *Alice in Wonderland*, and, though I never could finish the book, I loved to perform the first paragraph of *A Tale of Two Cities*.

Perhaps because of its notable symmetrical rhythm, "It was the best of times, it was the worst of times," or the dramatic list of contrasting circumstances, "It was the spring of hope, it was the winter of despair," I loved this paragraph and would read it over and over, even when I was alone in the back bedroom, staring out a window that looked over other houses, streets, a few palm trees, and a giant neon sign depicting red paint as it poured over a round earth, imagining as I read that I was creating a larger perspective on the urban scene below.

I did not know yet that with this practice I was training my ear to take in the music of language and, in the process, beginning to notice the music of the various phrases and sentences passing through my mind, bits and pieces, which even without any clear logic seemed to carry meaning. Over time I began to recognize these fragments as the seeds of something I might one day write.

Sound

When asked in an interview "how do stories begin for you?" one of the great storytellers of our time, Grace Paley, answered, "A lot of them begin with a sentence—they all begin with language."

We think of language as conveying meaning. But here, I believe, Paley is talking about sound as well as sense. "Very often," she goes on to say, "one sentence is absolutely resonant."

In this way, literature is not, as many often suppose, abstract. Its medium is the human voice, a phenomenon every bit as concrete and sensual as oil paint or marble from Carrara. And though modern attitudes do not recognize the meaning inherent in the concrete world, the medium is never passive. As Michelangelo told us, the material from which he sculpted his masterpieces guided him. "I saw the angel in the marble," he said, "and I carved until I set him free."

Sound can dive beneath presupposition and assumptions, the world of clichés that has already bored you, to unlock the vital yet undiscovered and unspoken worlds that lie just beneath the surface of what has become habitual.

For this reason, it is important that you listen to the words you have written. If the sound of your words is true (in the sense of a true note or hitting the mark), your reader will be riveted if not enchanted. And, more crucial to this process of writing, which you have already begun by this time, you will be exhausted; put in a kind of trance, the way religious ceremonies from diverse cultures have done for centuries. Thus, even you, as you write, will be led by the sound of the words you have written toward a wisdom you did not know you had within you.

The human voice is the world's most astonishing instrument, it's often said. It's capable of everything from a trill to a bark to an ear-splitting scream, from growling harmonics to liquid acrobatics, lofted on the breath like a lark on an updraft. Instrument is the wrong word, really. The voice is more like a chamber ensemble: winds and strings and blaring horns, strung together end to end. It's a pump organ, a viola, an oboe, and the bell of a trumpet, each instrument passing the sound along to the next, adding volume and overtones at every step. Throw in the percussion of the lips and the tongue, and the echoing amphitheatre of the skull, and you have a full orchestra playing inside you.

—BURKHARD BILGER, "Extreme Range"

PART II

Writing

Process

Nothing

By now you may have guessed that unless you are an unequaled practitioner of meditation, your mind is really never empty. Yet if you expect to find a whole novel, poem, essay, or play, you will be disappointed. What you will find, however, if you've learned to pay attention to your own thoughts, are bits and pieces, a sentence or two, even a paragraph, an image, a glimmer of something not yet born, but promising. But if they are to grow, these fragments must be tried and tested, written, fiddled with, erased, repeated, and rewritten on a page. And in this process, as you look for a path forward, you will be confronted with nothing countless times. Learn to see this recurring absence as potential, a space being made for what will come, because as you write, with each new paragraph or page or chapter, it is likely you will find yourself beginning again and again and again.

Yellow Lined Paper

Perfectionism is useful when you are on your final draft. But as you begin your work, the wish to be perfect can stop you from writing anything at all. At this stage, you might be throwing out at least half if not more of the words you write down. Using scrap paper or the yellow lined sheets on which you usually write notes or a grocery list will help loosen up your mood. This way you can avoid the pressure that comes from seeing your first attempt unfold in neat type on a screen. You don't have to come up with complete paragraphs or even sentences. A few words or phrases will do; perhaps the name of a song or a film will come to mind, an image you've seen somewhere or in your dreams. These fragments may seem like nothing. But they will form paths in your mind. It's more than likely that soon you will be able to follow these notes (like bread crumbs in a forest of thought) to map a path toward the meaning you are seeking.

What is crucial now is that you have taken some time to focus on the work you are in fact already creating, even if it's hardly detectable yet. This period of focus, no matter if it's only a quarter of an hour, will plant a seed in your mind that will germinate and grow of its own accord, so that suddenly, as you're driving your car or taking a walk or a bath or washing dishes, a full-blown concept will begin to emerge, or even a well-formed sentence. Don't forget to write these down. Such gifts are like the fruit that drops from a tree.

Catch them while you can. They deteriorate quickly.

Pause

This is a practice that will help at every stage of writing. Whenever you feel as if you don't know what to write next, pause, make a few notes, and then take a walk or a bath, or sleep on it. (Let the less conscious part of your mind take over.) Most often in this way a solution that had not occurred to you before will arrive.

Part of this practice involves what the psychologist George Leonard used to call "soft focus," which in this case means to hold a question or the end of a paragraph or a developing idea loosely in your mind.

I think of the old adage—that in order to write you must glue yourself to your desk chair for hours on end—as especially counterproductive. It may work for a journalist with a tight deadline, who has learned over time to produce quick results on demand, but for the rest of us, movement—simple physical movement, getting up out of your chair to make a cup of tea, for instance, or just standing and walking a few steps in order to look out the window—is an important part of the process. The body participates in thought, thinks, feels, responds, has opinions, makes decisions, is creative, and, if you listen, eventually turns silence into words.

There's an ocean of consciousness inside each of us, and it's an ocean of solutions. When you dive into that ocean, that consciousness, you enliven it. You don't dive for specific solutions; you dive to enliven that ocean of consciousness.

—DAVID LYNCH, *Catching the Big Fish*

Keeping Time

It can help to establish a regular schedule. Like a small child who will fall asleep more easily if put to bed at a regular time, your mind will be inclined to produce new ideas and words at the appointed hour.

In order not to feel overwhelmed, start with small increments, ten or fifteen minutes, during which you may write a sentence or two or simply think about your intended work. In this way you will be inviting rather than forcing the issue. Creativity is more like a cat than a dog. You can't order it to come to you. You just have to make yourself available until all of sudden you find it leaping into your lap.

Humble Work

The life of a writer is often portrayed as full of a certain bohemian glamour. And, of course, there are moments in most of our lives that qualify: sitting in the afternoon sun in Paris or some other city at an outdoor cafe drinking Kir or beer or coffee. But really, anyone can do that. What writers spend most of our time doing is sitting at a desk alone writing. Yes, there are dramatic moments of inspiration. Though these are usually hard earned, they do happen. Regarding the slow, humble work of choosing words, crafting sentences, paragraphs, and chapters, there is a story I often tell. I can't remember the source. I imagine I took part of it from the Brothers Grimm and added aspects from *One Thousand and One Nights*.

It goes like this. The local sultan or aristocrat, as it may be, hears that there is a shoemaker in town who makes very good shoes. This powerful man goes straightaway to the shop and, impressed with what he finds, tells the shoemaker that for one thousand new pairs of shoes, he will pay him a bag of gold, enough to make the shoemaker and his family rich. The shoemaker, who is having trouble making ends meet, is delighted. Until he hears the sultan say that the shoes must be ready by the morning, and if they are not, he will cut off the shoemaker's head.

After the potentate leaves, the shoemaker is, as you can imagine, distraught. Indeed, as he ponders the impossible task before him and thinks about his own fate, he begins to weep, especially when he thinks of his family, who, once he has perished, in this patriarchal land that offers no employment for women, are bound to starve to death.

There is no way he can make a thousand pairs of shoes overnight. But because he is just a humble shoemaker, he can think of nothing else to do but keep on cutting pieces of leather, shaping them to lasts, and sewing them together, one after another, doing what he knows how to do so well, crafting each pair carefully. By one in the morning, he has completed twenty pairs of shoes, a prodigious accomplishment for anyone, but of course nowhere near enough to satisfy the sultan. Nevertheless, he keeps laboring. Until around three in the morning, by which time he has made thirty pairs, he finds he no longer has the strength to work properly and decides to take a short nap. It is a nap that goes on almost until dawn. Sensing the impending sunrise, the cobbler awakes in a panic. He is certain now that he is doomed until, out of the corner of his eye, he glimpses several elves running from his workshop, leaving behind them, in neat rows, 970 pairs of excellent shoes, which, together with his thirty, will certainly satisfy the sultan.

The moral of the story? Writing is humble work. But if you keep at it with a slow and steady pace, the elves will eventually come, often showing up as you sleep, or take a walk, or stare out the window, giving you an astonishing insight or an exquisite turn that you had not anticipated, what you might call inspiration, a magical gift beyond your powers to summon or will.

But here is the trick: while you keep your faith in miracles, if you want the elves to come, remember to tend to your humble craft.

Walking

When, as you are writing, you encounter a problem or question for which you can think of no answer, among other strategies I have recommended, taking a walk is often the best ploy. Both metaphorically and actually, inspiration requires fresh air. (Note the root for inspiration, "inspire," which recalls the act of drawing a breath.) Any physical motion you undertake will literally oxygenate your whole body. Movement opens the doors and windows of your mind.

Perhaps this is why so many great works of literature have been fashioned around walking. There is the pilgrimage, for instance, that frames and provides the setting for Chaucer's *Canterbury Tales*, the metaphorical trail blazed by Dante in his *Divine Comedy*, the many books John Muir gave us describing his wide-ranging botanical adventures, a posthumous collection of Thoreau's essays aptly called *Walking*, or *The Songlines*, Bruce Chatwin's account of how walking is a spiritual practice in Aboriginal culture, and more recently Cheryl Strayed's *Wild*, or Rebecca Solnit's *Wanderlust*. Again, we must not forget the first volume of Proust's *In Search of Lost Time*, which was inspired and structured by a walk along that particular path called *Swann's Way*. And speaking of French literature, the many *flaneurs* (wandering walkers) that people Parisian poetry, from François Villon to Charles Baudelaire, come to mind.

Can it be that the reason this is such a frequent subject lies not only in the effectiveness of walking to summon creative thought but in the countless similarities between walking and writing?

The likeness is remarkable. It begins perhaps with what we call rhythm, which walking shares with literature. When speaking of physical ambulation, we call it a gait. Everyone has a unique gait, one that, as I grow older, I am acutely aware changes with age. Children seem to skip and play and almost run as they walk; tall, broad-shouldered people sometimes lumber; certain malevolent characters creep; those of us who are aging are known to shuffle at times. The gait is not inconsequential; it betrays inner states of mind and heart.

The same is true for gait in literature. We all know that poetry has a rhythm. But so does prose. And I suspect this is not only because grammar is rhythmic but because thought itself proceeds according to a beat. Think of it. Proposition. Argument. Proof. Conclusion. That could be a line from Cole Porter or rapper Jay-Z. And is it possible that the rhythm of thought and that of a walk mimic a basic rhythm in the body, which itself is tuned to the rhythm of the universe, patterns of time in nature, seasons, sunrise, noon, afternoon, sunset, night, all mirrored again in conscious thought and dreams?

Listen to the first clause of the second and most famous sentence of the Declaration of Independence: "We hold these truths to be self-evident."

Can you detect the rhythm?

We *hold* these *truths* to *be* self-*ev* i*dent*.

As with all rhythm in literature, this pattern creates an effect that is part of the meaning. It is as if Jefferson, or any representative of the thirteen colonies, were pounding his hand on the lectern (or stamping his foot) to emphasize the inarguable truth and justice of this declaration.

And speaking of feet, it can hardly be an accident that the term for a pair of syllables in poetry is "a foot," in the end another metaphor taken from walking.

Walking shares other features with writing, among them plot

or a narrative line which we experience during walks as direction and destination. Movement is at the heart of both walking and writing; as you move the story along, the plot thickens and things change. Just as while walking you may take a side road (perhaps to the left), a plot can take a sinister turn. (Indeed, the etymology tells us that *sinister* once meant "left.")

And there is this too. The unique point of view that belongs to all of us while we write is similar to the point of view of the walker. We watch, we observe, we take in what we are seeing, at times describing it in very intimate detail, but all the while (even when describing our own feelings) we are basically observers, travelers in different lands, or alongside houses, yards, fields, parks that do not belong to us, peering into the lives of others, or into our own memories, present as ourselves certainly but also not as ourselves, being there but also recording, at the slight psychological distance that the craft requires. Christopher Isherwood puts it very well in his famous *Berlin Stories* when he declares, "I am a camera."

And finally going outside to take a walk, paradoxically, allows you to travel inward; like birds released from their cages, your thoughts seem to wander more freely than they do indoors. As simultaneously you venture outward, you move inward too; you are not only the one who moves but the one who is moved, which you hope happens to you every day while you are writing too.

"How do you tackle writer's block?"

"The best two ways are to take a long, vigorous walk, the second is to write by hand."

—AMANDA BRAINERD,
INTERVIEWED BY *Lit Hub*

Searching

Writing is a bit like archaeology. Though instead of evidence from cultures that existed in the past, you are looking for signs of something that will exist in the future. Go over your notes. See if any of the stray words you've recorded suggest an idea or a feeling, a character, or the bare beginnings of a story, whether true or fictional. Then think about what the word or words signify to you. Or glue together the shards you've recovered into one or two sentences. And if you already have a few complete sentences, do these seem to call for a paragraph?

At this point it's better to suspend judgment about what you've written until the next day in your schedule. Then, in a process that you will likely be repeating again and again, look at what you have written with a slightly more jaundiced eye. If what you wrote the day before is not as good as you imagined it to be, don't worry. This is part of the process. The temptation is to reject it altogether. But instead work with it a bit. Tinker. Perhaps the insight you have is valuable but the language you've used doesn't quite convey its complexity. It takes effort to capture the full dimensions of consciousness with words. For one thing, if language affords countless possibilities for innovation, it also balances this capacity with a tendency to conserve standard phrases. You may find that you have adopted such phrases even though they do not really convey what you meant to say.

What is crucial is that you do not settle for less. Not less by anyone else's standards. Rather, less than the insight or vision or memory that inspires you. You are an intrepid explorer and alone in this particular adventure if only because you are the only one, so far, who can enter, explore, and write a report that portrays at all accurately what you have found in your own mind.

Rings True

Regarding accuracy, as the brilliant Australian actor Marta Dusseldorp expresses during an interview, "You can't for a second lie . . . No lying ever." The moment I heard these words, I recognized them. The same warning holds true for writers.

"But what if," I can hear the objection arise, "you are writing fiction? And isn't acting pretending anyway? Aren't they both ultimately lies?"

The answer is that truth in art is not the same as truth in science or a courtroom, which should reflect literal and external truth, backed by facts and data. Instead, much of contemporary art reflects inner truth, and often this can only be expressed through simulation.

Though to be accurate, in a certain sense, the simulation must itself become real. In the late nineteenth and early twentieth centuries, first actor Sarah Bernhardt and later the Russian director Stanislavski transformed the art of acting from a series of prescribed mannerisms and gestures into what the Russian director called "psychological experience," during which the actor is not just representing an emotion but is instead actually feeling it. To tell a *lie* in this sense would be to fake an emotion rather than experience it.

A similar process takes place in writing. Whether fiction or nonfiction, the art of creating literature asks you to describe what you have actually felt and experienced, or what you feel your character or subject has experienced, authentically. One is often tempted to fake it, that is, to write what you think you should write, what the received opinion or the usual story is. But the writing that results from this sort of dutiful dishonesty is usually very dull. Whereas telling the truth, as difficult as this may be at first, leads to writing that is often far more compelling.

While playing the role of a Holocaust survivor in the Australian television series *A Place to Call Home*, Dusseldorp rarely if ever cries. To begin with, whether in performance or in writing, crying can steal the emotion away from your audience. But more importantly, this can short-circuit the complex and often subtle layers of emotion that are experienced by the survivors of severe trauma.

In a number of his novels and stories that describe Paris during the decades that followed the Holocaust, novelist Patrick Modiano also forgoes tears. Indeed, he refers only sparsely to the terrible events that transpired during World War II. This restraint is part of what he is portraying: Paris, a city that as a result of collective trauma, terror, and guilt remained in those days, in many ways, numb.

Of course, you can try to think through what your true feelings are (as you will inevitably find yourself doing in any case). But writing itself can help you locate deeper and often less-than-conscious emotions. As you look for the right words to express this inner experience, you must become an exacting master. Instead of searching analytically, listen to the sound of your words to find out if they resonate. Let your inner experience be the tuning fork. You are not looking for the most pleasing or impressive words. You are searching for what rings true.

Little by Little

Many years ago, after I received a contract for my first book, *Woman and Nature*, I felt daunted by the task of completing it. While we were spending a few days in Vermont together, I confessed my wariness to my good friend Adrienne Rich, with whom I had been exchanging ideas, poems, and references. She had secured a contract for her first book of prose, *Of Woman Born*, a few months earlier, and had already written a chapter. After confessing that she felt the same wariness in the beginning, she told me what she had learned. "You don't write a book," she said, "you write a paragraph, or a page." (And then another one.)

June 6, 1893

. . . it is tolerably clear that, as regards complexity of action, it can be considerably improved. It can be improved with patience—it can be improved with resolution and devotion and above all it can be improved with *reflection*. The main little mass of it is there but something more is wanted—and I must take some quiet creative hour . . . to think that out. Little by little . . . the right thing will come.

—HENRY JAMES, *The Complete Notebooks*

Point of Entry

In the popular imagination, writers are absorbed with words. And it's also believed that words are always what come to a writer's mind first. But even though words are the ultimate medium, the entry point can be anything, the sound of a voice (rather than what is being said), the scene in which words may be spoken or that words may eventually describe, the bare bones of a plot involving someone missing, a chance meeting, a failed love affair, a story you heard, a rumor, a photo on the front page of a newspaper, a mediocre statue in a town square, a vague and hardly verbal yet compelling memory from childhood, the character of someone close to you or whom you hardly know but who is intriguing nonetheless, an image of anything, a formal table setting, a hummingbird hovering over the last leaf on a dead tree, a crying child huddled in a doorway, an old bicycle, a seventeenth-century building about to be destroyed, or it could be a pattern, visual or otherwise, an incipient literary form that pleases or excites you, or it may even be something in the process of creating the work that, without you knowing it, has already begun.

Where You Start Is Not Always Where You Begin

That is, you do not always start writing a book (or an essay or a poem) by writing the words that will occupy the first page. Whatever you start writing may well be placed somewhere else, for instance in the middle, or even at the end. When I wrote *Woman and Nature*, among the first sections I wrote was the ending. The ending had an almost spiritual force, one which I soon realized the pages that came before would have to earn. In the same way, if an ending comes to you early in your process, it will tell you a great deal about what you will have to do to get there.

The challenge of beginnings might almost be described as the major challenge of writing anything at all. This is not because beginnings are so difficult. Sometimes they are and sometimes not. Rather it is because while writing anything, a twelve-line poem, an essay, a thousand-page novel, you are so often searching for beginnings. Not only each chapter but each paragraph has to have a beginning line. If a paragraph expands what you've written in the paragraph above it, that will not be so hard. But very often you will be changing direction slightly, tacking to the east or the west, feeling for the direction of the wind, trying to adjust your sails to accommodate both the weather and your intended destination.

You'll know that the beginning is working well when it seems to invite you to continue. I don't mean here that it has to be inviting as in the sense of charming. It does however need to send you along a fruitful route; whether those fruits be conceptual, emotional, or sensual doesn't matter. (And if it sends you along it will do that to the reader too.)

A first line can be simple, informative, and unpretentious, as in the opening sentence of the second chapter of Mary Shelley's classic tale, *Frankenstein*: "I spent the following day roaming through the valley." This sentence acts as a bridge leading us into the valley, which quickly, in the narrator's description, takes on a slightly ominous tone that is an augur of things to come, as Shelley writes, "the icy wall of the glacier overhung me."

The ways in which you can begin a book, or a chapter, or a paragraph are endless. To name just a few, some creative works or passages or paragraphs begin with a unique and compelling voice, some with a characteristic sound—whether melodious or rough or even grating—some with an element of a plot soon to develop, an image, a metaphor, the description of a scene, or of a character, some by discussing the process in which you are engaged.

Anything goes. As long as you don't bore yourself.

Fresh

The reason why so many seasoned writers suggest that you carry a notebook at all times is of course that you might forget a sentence you've crafted in your mind or a new thought or turn in your plot that has come to you when you are away from your desk. But there is another reason too. Especially when you're writing poetry, but often with prose too, you'll want to capture the exact words that have come to you. Too often, when you try to reformulate the words you've forgotten, some indefinable magic will be lost. As Walt Whitman said, "By writing at the instant the very heartbeat of life is caught."

Aikido

The approach at the heart of aikido is to use your opponent's energy for your own ends. If, for instance, you are a small woman being assaulted by a strong man, as he lunges at you, you can easily defeat him by seeming to receive rather than fight him, a move that throws him off balance, giving you, despite your size, a considerable advantage.

The same technique can be applied to problems you confront while writing. Suppose for example that as a narrative from your childhood unwinds itself first in your mind and then on the page, and you describe each member of your family, with all their ages and other details down to the color of their eyes, even what they liked to wear, you realize that to tell a certain very funny (or sad) story you've got to include your third cousin on your father's side. But how old was he and what did he look like? You can't remember. Nor can your siblings, nor even your father, whose memory is failing. You don't really even have this fellow's last name. You might consult a genealogist, except without his last name, you would not recognize it on any family tree. Other than the memory of a single summer afternoon that occurred over forty years ago, when you were just seven years old, he seems to have vanished from your world.

To employ aikido in this instance would be to write about your search for the identity of this "cousin" and the mystery that is left in the wake of your failure to learn anything more. Was he real? A figment of your imagination? Not really family? Or was there a family secret that kept him slightly veiled? And why do you remember him at all? As your inquiry develops, he will become far more interesting than if you had been able to simply write "Danny wore blue overalls that matched his blue eyes."

If it is not memory but words that fail you, you can use that too. Rebecca Solnit's work is full of extraordinarily evocative descriptions of cities and landscapes. So when she writes, "On the most beautiful days, there are no words for the colors of San Francisco Bay and the sky above it," we believe her and are stricken with awe as we imagine a beauty that exceeds the power of language.

A number of potential failures can be turned to your advantage as you write. When M. F. K. Fisher wrote about an incident with a scorpion bite that she witnessed while visiting a farm in Provence, she could not translate the formula for the herbal cure that her hostess called out in Provençal rhymes. "I cannot rhyme it in my own language," she tells us. Enough said. In this form, couched in the writer's inability, it will take up a rich place in the reader's imagination.

The same tactic can help you when you're reluctant to tell a story for fear it might embarrass a colleague, friend, or family member, or cause formidable anger. Say that when for a brief period your cousin was unemployed he had a nervous breakdown. Instead of describing details that might identify him, you might write that you are hiding the identity of the story's subject and then use the bare bones of the story itself to discuss the shame too often attached both to mental suffering and, not coincidentally, to unemployment.

On the other hand, while you are writing you may feel overwhelmed yourself by shame, embarrassment, and perhaps ambivalence about revealing this. The solution in these cases is not to suppress your emotions but to use them. Rather than fight with yourself, write about your shame or your fear. You can always cut passages you do not want to be public. But remember that whatever feelings you have will be very compelling to readers, not from prurient interest, but because so often they have had the same experience and felt conflicted in a similar way.

Then again, your difficulty in telling the story might not be personal at all but instead something you've encountered in the process of research or writing. But that too is a story you can tell. Several years after *The Boston Globe* revealed that the Catholic hierarchy had covered up widespread sexual abuse perpetrated by Catholic priests in Boston, *Spotlight*, a film based on the difficulties reporters encountered while trying to uncover the truth, won the Oscar for Best Picture.

Whatever the problem is that you encounter in writing, it will help you to get past it if you write about it. If you haven't written a word in two months, write about that. Begin with the very simple sentence, "I haven't written a word in two months." More often than not this unlocks several other sentences at least.

In this way, instead of fighting the force, whatever it is, that is blocking you, you have joined forces *with* it. And if you explore your experience closely and deeply enough, you may be writing something valuable to readers, because whatever is censored, and along with that, censorship itself, is often the most fascinating part of any story.

Writing requires self-reflection, what you might call a habit of awareness together with a shift from perfectionism, or a fear of failure, to a keen interest in whatever is bothering you. A slight movement of mind from worry or fear to curiosity makes all the difference.

Another cure I learned on the farm near Aix was for bad insect bites. It was the kind of rune in the dialect that Gaby the farmer's wife used, part Provençal and part Piedmontese, but I can't rhyme it in my own language.

She sang it out in a rough shout when her husband came running into the courtyard from the olive orchard, rolling up his trouser-leg as he stumbled along. He yelled something at her and "A scorpion bite . . . he's been bitten," she cried out. She yelled, then, the rhyme at us, and when we did not understand she ran off herself and came straight back with a handful of leaves . . .

—M. F. K. FISHER, *A Cordiall Water*

A Reading List of Your Own

Of course, you'll want to read the classic texts on your subject. But you might be drawn in less predictable directions too. You never know what you'll learn along the way. Follow your nose. Read whatever most interests you.

(How I Learned to Write)

My sister was the instigator behind the trips we made to the legendary Pickwick Book Shop on Hollywood Boulevard. Since I relished all the limited time I spent with her, this famous bookstore took on an almost sacred dimension for me. If in the beginning I would tag along to whatever shelves she visited, after a while I began to develop my own tastes. What I liked best was wandering among the shelves of used books, even on the top floor in the hallowed rare book section, where once I was thrilled to find Aldous Huxley peering at a yellowing manuscript through his very thick glasses.

It was an initiation into the world of literature, which, as I picked up one volume after another, seemed like an echo chamber where a choir dwelled, made of a diverse range of voices, cries, whispers, and insolent laughter, sometimes telling shameful secrets, often leavened by the habit of reflection. But it was also a meeting place, where different forms and genres, movements, and styles shared the same space, bathed in an attitude of respect that held the oldest, Dante or Sappho, and the most recent during those days—Dylan Thomas or Mary McCarthy—in the same regard.

Continuing my informal education, I studied several anthologies, pages through which I discovered a wildly disparate mélange of writers, from Lorca to Rimbaud and Langston Hughes, Fitzgerald and Hemingway to Dorothy Parker, Marianne Moore, Gertrude Stein, and Eudora Welty, taking in all the various sounds of what was then called "modern" literature, and along the way learning some of the fundamentals of literary form.

This immersion must have initiated an alchemical process

within me, because just as I began to be able to recognize those forms, I began to write short stories and poetry myself.

It was only a year or two later, after I entered high school, that I found a group of like-minded friends. We would gather on a Saturday night around a coffee table on which, in order to create a bohemian atmosphere, we had placed a candle that we coaxed to drip over an old wine bottle, as we read our favorite poems by W. H. Auden or Dylan Thomas, William Carlos Williams or T. S. Eliot to each other. Later on, we danced to recordings of Fats Domino or Chuck Berry. Music which, along with the poems we read, must have made its way into what we wrote and published in the journals that, decades before personal computers existed, we published with the use of mimeograph machines and distributed among friends and fellow students.

Just two years before the advent of the revolutionary sixties, ours was an intellectual rebellion. I still have a vivid memory of the day my friends and I cut school and drove over the hills into Hollywood so we could spend the day together at Pickwick Book Shop, the sincerest form of revolution we could imagine perpetrating.

Material Worlds

Words

Language is fossil poetry.
—RALPH WALDO EMERSON, "The Poet"

Words provide the raw material of writing. Though to say "raw" here seems a bit misleading. If anything in human consciousness can be considered well cooked, it would be vocabulary. Most words have a long history, trailing back in time and over space to diverse, often ancient cultures. For example, you can trace the word *word* through old English to German, Dutch, Old Norse, and Latin roots, all the way back to what archaeologists call Proto-Indo-European, a language spoken in the Bronze Age, six thousand years ago.

Every word you use echoes back in time through a shared history. You don't have to do anything about it, except it will greatly enrich your process to listen for the resonances, of which every word has many, some etymological and others connotative. Most words carry countless associations, some cultural and others personal. For instance, when I hear the word *word*, a rush of references arises in my mind, ranging from a tune written in the thirties called "Three Little Words," to the phrase "at a loss for words," to the memory of my granddaughter's first words.

With each word you choose, its connotations, whether invited or not, will come along too. But even though you may not be fully conscious of the associations each word carries, or perhaps because of those, when you are choosing words, trust your natural, often less than conscious inclinations, which themselves are influenced by associations. Don't settle for a word simply because it has the correct dictionary definition. It must feel right too.

A corollary to this is that while it may be a good idea to expand your vocabulary, when you find a new word, in most cases it's wise to wait before you use it until you really understand its connotative meanings, including the contexts in which it is usually spoken. Though at times discovering a new word will allow you to understand something you know or have experienced with a new clarity. In her autobiographical essay, "A Sketch of the Past," Virginia Woolf describes her first encounter with the word *ambivalence*. Speaking of her feelings toward her father, she writes, "in me . . . rage alternated with love. It was only the other day when I read Freud, for the first time, that I discovered that this violently disturbing conflict of love and hate is a common feeling; and it is called ambivalence."

It's easy to use common phrases when you write, and even at times preferable, where they fit or are accurate. (If you are constantly striving to be inventive, not only will you wear yourself out, your reader will soon get tired too.) And, speaking of "fresh," it's important that as you write, you listen to the language you are using with fresh ears. Recently linguist George Lakoff suggested to activists regarding the issue of student debts that they forgo the habitual phrase, which is to *forgive debts*, and use the phrase *cancel debts* instead. While this campaign argues that students should not be forced to incur debt in order to be educated, the use of the word *forgive* implies that having debt is a sin. Employing a habitual phrase, the organizers had failed to really hear what their words implied.

Be aware too of the sound of words, not only each word by itself but in relation to the sounds that surround it. When you write you are also constantly composing a kind of music. Though many think, erroneously, of writing as abstract, words have a sensual power through the sounds they make. And as such, they are part of the material world. Think of the word *word*. The W in this case is somewhat drawn out, expansive, requiring you to thrust your lips outward, and when combined with the O that follows, glances off the supernatural (as in "woo-woo") before landing firmly in RD, recalling Urdu, a language rich in mystical texts, while cunningly rhyming with "heard," and then coming down to earth, of which it even seems, through the grinding sound of *rrrd*, to penetrate the surface.

Some words very clearly echo the sound of whatever they represent. This practice is called onomatopoeia. My favorite example of this is the French word for the sound a cat makes when it purrs, *ronronner*, pronounced "rhonrrrunnaye," which when the *rr*s are rolled, as French requires, sounds like a cat when it purrs.

Just as the captain of a ship must have a feel for water, a writer has to develop a feel for words. Perhaps this is why, when I was young, so many would-be writers, myself included, committed Lewis Carroll's "Jabberwocky" to memory. Constructed from nonsense syllables, this poem sent us on a journey through which we learned a great deal about meaning and sound. The lines "All mimsy were the borogoves, / And the mome raths outgrabe," ring in my ears even now, making me laugh, a laughter still filled with wonder at the ways of words.

That effect of colour has real power . . . so much power that, in certain lights, it seems to become a substance . . .

—HENRI MATISSE (AS QUOTED BY
JOHN CHRISTIE IN JOHN BERGER'S
I Send You This Cadmium Red)

Inside a Word

Sometimes, inside a word, you can find another word that will inspire you and perhaps enlarge the circumference of your thoughts, or lend support to ideas you have been developing. In an essay entitled "They Think They Can Bully the Truth," Rebecca Solnit notes that the word *dictator* is related to the word *dictate*.

"There are among us," she writes, "people who assume their authority is so great they can dictate what happened," despite any facts to the contrary.

One can also make more fanciful associations. In the seventies, as the women's movement reached a fever pitch, the word *herstory* was invented. It was effective for a period at least, even though the word *history* comes from *histoire*, the French word for history, and not from, as was implied, "his story."

Picture the Word

> The difference between the almost right word and
> the right word is . . . the difference between the
> lightning bug and the lightning.
>
> —MARK TWAIN

Picture the words you use. Do you want to say *blunt* or *impede*? They are both unfortunate actions, at least if you are the one being blunted or impeded, but the first seems soft whereas the other is harder and sounds vaguely legal, like a traffic barrier, from which, in case you should crash into it, you would no doubt be injured. For the word *blunt* the thesaurus I use has listed several synonyms, among them *soften, dull, take the edge off, numb, stupefy, deaden, weaken, impair, devitalize, appease, mollify.* But none of these are the same exactly as *blunt.* You would not want to try to *stupefy* the cutting edge of an axe, or for that matter to *deaden* it. (Even if it could deaden you.) And though axes have edges, *take the edge off* would not be right either. Words call up images. And they have associations. Such as, she *took the edge off* a day of hard work with a second glass of red wine.

Metaphor

There is something very pleasing about metaphors. With the use of a metaphor, one thing is made to stand for another. Can the appeal of this device be attributed to the fact that the stand-in is most often three-dimensional, as it were, *in the flesh*? Whether from fable or life on earth, metaphors make concrete and vivid what otherwise might be relatively pale statements of fact or, worse, unclear conjectures.

Think of this chilling statement from Sophocles's *Oedipus Rex*: "Time, which sees all things, has found you out." Here time is personified as an omniscient detective or a hunter on the chase, who has found his (or her) prey. The use of metaphor here has the effect of creating a dramatic narrative within one sentence, in this case, conjuring a drama within a drama. Time becomes a less menacing though rather arrogant character in Walter Benjamin's *Berlin Childhood Around 1900*, where he writes, "In my room I waited until 6 o'clock deigned to arrive." What matters here is that in both cases time has become human.

Other metaphors bring the human into the animal realm. In Homer's account, when the Trojans leap into battle, they do so with cries and shouts like cranes. In every case, two things or beings usually thought to be separate and different, both existentially and philosophically, are equated.

In Edith Wharton's *The Age of Innocence*, describing his conflicted state of mind, Newland Archer conjures a vivid drama: "Once more it was borne in on him that marriage was not the safe anchorage he had been taught to think, but an uncharted voyage on the seas." Though this imagery may feel exaggerated, it captures how precarious the situation feels to Archer.

Virginia Woolf does something similar, as she describes the inner life of a character in her novel *To the Lighthouse*: "And again she felt alone in the presence of her old antagonist, life," personifying "life" as a persistent villain. A paradoxical metaphor, similar to one that Toni Morrison uses in *Beloved*, speaking of extreme feelings brought on by extreme injustice: "More than the rest, they killed the flirt whom folks called Life for leading them on."

Our language is replete with phrases that are metaphorical. From the lovely "blanketed in snow" to the very odd "raining cats and dogs" to the almost invisible "pave the way to" or "open the door to," our minds are constantly being occupied by images "handed down" to us from generations of speakers.

If you study etymology, the inheritance is even larger than that. Almost all the seemingly abstract words we commonly use were once names for material things. Who would have guessed, for instance, that the word *truth* evolved from the word for *tree*. (In particular a straight tree, used no doubt to measure lengths of various materials.)

Metaphors are like very short stories. Despite all the sophisticated tools we have invented, including email and cell phones, when we seek to communicate or understand clearly, we often use earthly symbols, even as a way to reach for the stars.

It Cannot Be Named

There is a central quality, which is the root crite-
rion of life and spirit . . . This quality is objective
and precise, but it cannot be named.

—CHRISTOPHER ALEXANDER,
The Timeless Way of Building

When there is no word for what you have experienced, felt, or observed, you will have to capture it obliquely: with metaphor, by
surrounding it with words, or by describing what surrounds it with
words. As elusive as such subjects are, attempts to describe them
create some of the best writing, perhaps because, as irresistible as
such attempts can be, the meaning of life itself is also very hard to
pin down.

The Goddess

She passes often through
the empty sleep of noon
leaving no trace
of a body.
But when nature senses her,
this habit of secrecy
lends a terrible clarity
to the touching sweetness
of her shape.

—RAINER MARIA RILKE,
FROM HIS FRENCH POEMS
(TRANS. SUSAN GRIFFIN)

Sentences

I want the language of lovers
before they touch,
when their eyes telegraph
verbs only, because
each word costs.

—CHANA BLOCH, "Crossing the Table"

Sentences are like rivers. They flow, move you to tears, bring you to see, or simply mirror the constant movement of life. No wonder. The heart of a sentence, without which it cannot be called a sentence, is a verb: a verb by definition is a word that describes or embodies action.

A collection of words, no matter how many there are, does not make a sentence. If I write, "Grammar in my education, in the state of California, 1950, in an old-fashioned way, in a word boring," I have not created a sentence. However, if I add a verb, "Grammar in my education, in the state of California, 1950, *was taught* in an old-fashioned way, in a word boring," I have a sentence.

By including a subject and a verb, a sentence tells us who did what and, if I add an object, to whom or what. Each sentence is a narrative unto itself. It evolves; it moves, if only toward a logical conclusion. And it also travels off the page, from somewhere in your mind to somewhere in the mind of the reader. (Think of the phrase *train of thought*.) Just as the songs, poems, essays, novels, and stories built from sentences are shaped by actions, including emotions, evolving ideas, and events, the sentence itself is an action in progress.

Can this be why the process of composing sentences is so often transformational? To craft a sentence will change not only what you write, but most often, if even on a very subtle scale, your own thoughts.

What transforms the writer is not catharsis, as in therapy, but craft. Like language itself, craft has been inherited across many languages and cultures and over several millennia. In earlier cultures, the storyteller was also a shaman or spiritual leader of some kind, and the storyteller's art, or craft, carried an intrinsic wisdom, which along with stories has been passed down to us through countless generations. When you craft your language, which you are doing as soon as you begin to write a sentence, you are never alone; you are working in tandem with ancient teachers from diverse cultures, societies, gatherings, meetings, rituals, lineages, not to speak of the volumes and volumes written before you began to write, all part of the host that hums around language.

Grappling with the craft of forming a lucid sentence, you may become aware of aspects of your subject you had not noticed before, and in this way, your vision will be expanded. Or your struggle with syntax may reveal that, without intending it, you have not been entirely accurate. (Misshapen prose can obscure many kinds of errors.) You may in this regard realize that instead of syntax or vocabulary, there is a contradiction or flaw in your thinking that is muddling your sentence. Moreover, as you structure your sentence, you must locate the center of your story or idea and by the same stroke identify what is either an aspect of your subject, or tangential to it.

In order to experience this alchemy, while you are constructing sentences, remain open, if even on a subtle level, to learning something new. Writing is not only about what you know; it is a journey filled with discovery.

There is no hard and fast rule about how long a sentence ought to be or how much information it ought to convey. Except that it's wise to listen to what you have wrought. Read it aloud. Feel the sound. At times a long sentence can feel cluttered, like a room filled with too much furniture or too many things crowding a tabletop. Pay attention to your own energy. Do you feel a sudden fatigue when you read certain unwieldy sentences? Or do you find yourself rushing through it, as if this is an onerous task?

Most often, when I detect an error or a failing in a sentence I have written or in a manuscript I am editing, I do so with my ear. I sense through sound that something isn't right. Or as we say, *it doesn't sound right*. Only after I tinker with the sentence can I determine what the problem is.

Among its many incarnations, a sentence is a stream of sounds. Listen to the rhythm in this simple sentence from Elizabeth Rosner's novel, *The Speed of Light*: "He looked at me and I knew he didn't see me." The repetition here is not mistaken but instead creates music, as does the rhyme between "see" and "me." Just as words have an undertow of connotations, so do sentences, beneath their meanings, have an undertow of music. If you have created enough silence around you and listen inwardly while you work, you might well find yourself creating such patterns, even a kind of onomatopoeia.

The sound of an effective sentence is not arbitrary. Rather, it reflects the process of thought itself. Listen to the mournful sentence that begins James Baldwin's novel, *Giovanni's Room*:

> I stand at the window of this great house in the south of France as night falls, the night which is leading me to the most terrible morning of my life.

While the movement of this sentence foretells the inexorable movement of time, in sound as well as content, it also mirrors the narrator's mind, filled with the particular angst that is inspired by memories of events that cannot be changed. And its remarkable beauty is allied to the accuracy with which it captures the moment it describes.

As soon as a sentence calls attention to itself, demonstrates how clever the author is, how astute, how talented, I know something's gone wrong. The writer is no longer at the service of the words, the words are serving the writer. Each sentence needs to be entirely necessary to the work as a whole, and yet each sentence needs to be full of humility. A sentence that seeks to dazzle is merely annoying. A sentence that dazzles even as it deflects our amazement, graciously leading us to the next, is a sentence worth keeping.

—ALICE McDERMOTT,
"The Art of Fiction No. 244,"
The Paris Review

And Hemingway

Hemingway is known for his frequent use of the word *and*. This single syllable became both the hallmark and the foundation of his style. Like a constant drumbeat, marking time with a single note, this simple conjunction forges several different but related actions into one long movement, making a music that we recognize almost immediately as Hemingway's.

> I loved to take her hair down and she sat on the bed and kept very still, except suddenly she would dip down to kiss me while I was doing it, and I would take out the pins and lay them on the sheet and it would be loose and I would watch her while she kept very still and then take out the last two pins and it would all come down and she would drop her head and we would both be inside of it, and it was the feeling of inside a tent or behind a falls.

Again and again he pulls off what feels almost like magic, while, as reading a passage from one of his novels, we are drawn into wells of feeling.

The simple beat of "and" works in tandem with Hemingway's embrace of plain American speech, a decision adopted by a larger literary movement that included his friend Gertrude Stein. The sound of language that came from that movement is with us still.

Hemingway's style is intoxicating. Hearing it, you may be tempted to adopt it yourself. A word to the wise, though: what he achieves is not as mechanical as it seems. He builds a powerful emotional narrative from a careful sequence of small actions, masterfully. But unless you want to sound like a cliché, be careful about imitating Hemingway's prose. The repeated use of "and" can be tedious. Let his example be just one among many in the flexible, seemingly infinite universe of possibilities you have been given or that you may discover on your own as a writer.

Prepositions

Above, across, along, at, before, below, beyond, by, for, from, in, inside, into, over, to, toward, upon, with, within. They are very small. Why worry about them at all? Because, simply stated, the wrong one can make your writing sound awkward.

They are, however, easy to fix. But since there is often no rhyme or reason why certain prepositions are used with certain verbs to convey particular meanings, logic cannot be relied upon to solve this problem. Often there is no clear reason why you should write "to" Mr. Abercrombie and not "at" him, though while you can say he lives "at" 2020 Charing Cross Road, it is evident why you should not say that he lives "in" 2020 Charing Cross Road (which implies he's eccentric if not in danger).

Though certainly prepositions provide an orientation, they are also the result of habits in language best not broken, unless you have a good reason to do that. (If, for instance, Mr. Abercrombie is indeed stubbornly living in the middle of the road.)

Prepositions can convey subtle meanings. The difference between "speak to" and "speak with," for example, is primarily emotional. "Speak to" implies a hierarchy, as in "I will speak to the janitor about the dust," whereas "speak with" implies a more democratic relationship: "Let me speak with the janitor about that." (Though, depending on the context and the tone, speaking "with" can also indicate a disciplinary warning.)

Similarly, to speak "of" has several meanings, ranging from speaking highly "of" your friend the florist to speaking "of the devil." Each preposition points to a particular meaning. To speak "out" can be courageous but to speak "out of turn" can be boorish. As for speaking "to," you may be addressing someone or you may be addressing, or talking about, a subject or a question, as in the Speaker of the House spoke "to" the question of impeachment.

As with so many skills writers should develop, the more you read, the more you will inherit and imbibe the habitual use of prepositions.

Long Sentences

Warning: these require a great deal of skill. It is very easy to botch them, though when they are successful, they are admirable.

When it comes to fashioning sentences, grammar is not the only consideration. A sentence is a unit of meaning. But it is also a piece of music, with a harmonious tempo that is not, at the same time, so repetitive as to be dull. The task is to know (or to discover, as you are writing) the relationship, as you see it, of one idea, feeling, sensation, or thing to another and to make certain the sentence mirrors those relationships in proximity, proportionality, and music as well as, of course, sense.

Try it. Even if you fail, you will learn a great deal.

Clutter

Sometimes a sentence can seem like an obstacle course, as if instead of driving along an unobstructed road, you have had to cope with a series of detours. Ask yourself if these detours are really necessary. As you write, all kinds of second thoughts and interesting associations will occur to you. But to the reader many of these will only obscure the meaning of your sentence. This is especially true whenever what you are describing is complex or complicated.

Stein's Sentences

... what remains is a sense of someone's having built.

—JOHN ASHBERY

Something wondrous happens when you read Gertrude Stein. You feel that she is making perfect sense. This is a feeling more than a thought, perhaps even a physical feeling. Her sentences are structured so that they travel through your bones in a familiar way. They sound just like the patterns in which sense is usually wrapped. For instance:

A sentence. It is a beautiful day and satisfactory.
A sentence. With what will they think about what
    they will have to have.
A sentence. It is by the time that they are furnished
    that they will find it pleasant to do it.

But when these sentences have landed in your mind, you will be confounded. They do not really make sense. Still, they sound so simple, so right, like clear directions from a reliable speaker. You trust this voice.

How does she do this? I will not try to answer this question, nor will I engage in either literary exegesis or hermeneutics here. I only wish to point out that while in "Jabberwocky" Lewis Carroll mimics words, here Stein mimics, successfully, grammar. In a chapter called "Sentences," from her book *How to Write*, she puts common phrases together in a manner that creates the familiar structure of complete sentences, rhythms most of us learned to recognize even before we knew any words, when we were infants.

If Stein's work does anything, it illustrates the great power of those patterns.

Throughout her work, masked as familiarity, the sound of language comes unmoored from sense. This rupture may make you very nervous, or it may make you laugh. For the latter effect, it's best to read her work out loud, with an authoritative tone.

> A sentence is made by coupling meanwhile ride
>   around
> to be a couple there makes grateful dubiety named
>   atlas
> coin in a loan.
> This is what they all do

Paragraphs

Two blocks away from my home, along the route that, several times a week, I usually walk, a house is being remodeled. The crew has taken down all the stucco walls so that only the wooden structure remains. I doubt I am alone in this fascination. For some reason I love to see the structure of a house be revealed and to watch as gradually a home is built or rebuilt from the bare bones.

Like architecture, literature requires structure. Before they are arranged into sentences, words alone do not provide structure. Rather, they are like the material—lumber or steel or concrete—used in construction. Sentences certainly have structure. But beginning with paragraphs, you start to see the work as a whole come into being.

As with a completed work, most paragraphs have a beginning, middle, and end. In the same way that, in order to provide meaning, the words within a sentence are ordered, so the meaning and impact of a paragraph is created by the order as well as the content of its sentences. Another way of saying this is that it is not only the literal meaning of a sentence but where it is placed that will determine its effect. The sentences within a paragraph are no longer separate. They act together as a unit.

Accordingly, paragraphs are not just created by random indentations. They can in fact be of various lengths, and even at times be just one sentence long. A word or an exclamation. A quarter page. Or several pages. What makes a paragraph a paragraph is not length but content. They are units of meaning. And they should be choreographed to convey that meaning.

A paragraph that is placed eleven pages into the first chapter of Patti Smith's *Just Kids* begins with the sentence, "I had no proof that I had the stuff to be an artist, though I hungered to be one." This sentence frames what is to follow, where she tells us that one night while watching a film called *The Song of Bernadette* on television, she learned that the young saint never asked to be *called*. This worried her, she tells us, before ending the paragraph: "I didn't mind the misery of a vocation but I dreaded not being called."

How a paragraph ends is as important as how it begins. Exploring the development of her wish to be an artist, this paragraph is complete in itself. While avoiding any pat answers, and leaving the question open, it gives a full description of her fervent desire to be an artist, allowing her and the reader to jump to a new subject in the next paragraph that begins, "I shot up several inches."

The space before a paragraph starts and after it ends defines a paragraph, and it is as much an element of communication as the words that are used. In both poetry and prose, empty space is a sign with many different meanings, telegraphing a slight pause, a sigh, an intake of breath, a bridge, a disconnection or different direction, suspense, an unanswered question, appreciation, along with countless other messages, or simply an end. What you need to remember as a writer is that this space is seldom neutral. And that it gives you another tool. But space alone does not make a paragraph. A paragraph must develop, either through physical action or the changes that occur in hearts and minds.

As with any form that survives through time, the range of aesthetic and cognitive choices that paragraphs offer seems infinite. Among the possibilities within that range is the idea that a paragraph can be an entire work unto itself. Prose poetry and flash fiction use paragraphs this way. As does Claudia Rankine's powerful work, *Citizen: An American Lyric*, which is made up of paragraphs that could stand alone as stories, prose poems, and essays all at once, but that put together are even more powerful than they are apart. Her form mirrors her subject matter, the way that racism gathers the cumulative power to do significant harm from thousands of seemingly separate, small incidents. As she writes, "Certain moments send adrenaline to the heart, dry out the tongue and clog the lungs."

As you are crafting a paragraph, certain features of the whole manuscript will arise. You can see and feel how voice, tone, person, focus, style, the verb tense you have chosen—past, present, or future—come together, forming a whole entity, almost like a living creature, with ways of being, characteristic responses, and a will of its own.

At times writers make such choices logically but more often they come to us after immersing ourselves in the subject matter, after breathing the subject in, walking with it, sleeping on it, letting it into our dreams, coaxing it phrase by phrase into language. Sometimes, if we have pondered what approach to take for several hours or days or even weeks, the work starts to speak to us. And the product of that monologue is, more often than not, a paragraph.

Making It Whole

Building

As thrilling as it is to fly through literary space unimpeded by any plans, writing with no immediate structure in mind might seem foolish. And no doubt it would be, if you were writing a report to the city on traffic congestion. But when you are pursuing the wisp of an idea or following the scent of a story, contriving to build a structure prematurely can cut you off from unanticipated turns and twists of significance. If you settle on a structure too early it is likely to be a cookie-cutter form, what is expected, the usual thing. But if you let the work reveal its structure to you gradually, even if it is not unique, the structure will be an integral part of the meaning. And like anything tailor-made, it will fit perfectly.

There are countless structures (including many, no doubt, that have not yet appeared in literature). None, as far as I can see, are any better than any other. The question is what will best serve your work. Let the work tell you that. (But it helps in this case too, as with all tasks that a writer faces, if you have read widely, at least in your chosen form.)

One of the most common structures is that provided by time, probably because narrative is tied to chronology, as in this happened and then that did, in which more than likely at least a hint of causation is implied. Yet the direction in which the chronology of events in a story is headed is not a given. The whole book can be a flashback in time. You can also flash forward in the middle of a narrative. You can weave in and out of different periods of time. Or you can, as I did in *A Chorus of Stones*, move backward in time.

In writing an essay it is common to begin with a proposition or a political position and then outline the reasons why this is true (at least in the author's eyes). The argument for a thesis may well include one or several stories, proffered as either examples or informal proof or both. In this case a chronology may lie within each story. (And another kind of plot, the formation of an idea, also develops over time.)

A work can also be schematic, step by step covering aspects of a given subject, as in rooms of a house, moving perhaps from the common meeting place, the salon or living room, to, eventually, the most private, as in bedrooms.

The structure is tied, of course, to voice and subject matter and will come out of these almost naturally if you allow it to age properly.

One way to know that you have found the right structure is that it is generative. It can guide you to new insights about your subject or about the work itself. Another sign that a structure is right is that it facilitates rather than impedes your work. In this and so many other ways the Calvinist work ethic—"roll up your sleeves"—is counterproductive. It helps to think of the structure of a given work as less a task to complete than a phenomenon to be detected. Very often writers begin a work with no idea of what the plot will be. To cite a famous example, Simone de Beauvoir tells us in an interview with *The Paris Review*, "I start writing a novel long before working out the plot."

Whenever they are conceived, the right form, structure, and voice will inspire if not compel you toward the next page.

He loved detective novels. He found in their formulae the ideal narrative structures which allow the fiction writer to set up his own borders and to concentrate on the efficiency of words. He enjoyed significant details. He once observed, as we were reading the Sherlock Holmes story "The Red-Headed League," that detective fiction was closer to the Aristotelian notion of a literary work than any other genre . . . that in the detective story, the unity is given by the mystery itself.

—ALBERTO MANGUEL, *With Borges*

Framing Lines

Framing lines should occur throughout your piece, providing structure for each paragraph (or passage or chapter). A framing line will usually be the first sentence (though at times it occurs in second or even third place). Such sentences focus the attention of readers on the subject at hand so that they will read whatever they encounter subsequently in that light.

Here is a line that begins a paragraph, a sentence that occurs in the middle of a book by Diane Johnson called *The True History of the First Mrs. Meredith, and Other Lesser Lives*: "The Historian cannot capture a process so slow as the death of a marriage."

The lines that follow tell us, in Johnson's estimation, why and how it should be the case that marriages dissolve too slowly to describe. Referring obliquely both to biographers in general and to herself as "the Historian," with a capital "H," also sets the tone of what is to come, a tone that is both sympathetic and at the same time ironic and witty.

Framing lines are often composed after the fact, that is, after you have written at least part of the paragraph or passage you want to frame, when it has become more evident what the subject is that you wish to introduce. To paraphrase a line from "The Waking," a famous poem by Theodore Roethke, you learn by going where you have to go.

Transitions

Once you have one or more paragraphs that address the same subject or depict a common scene, you may want to change the subject, in which case you will need to create a transition.

A transition is like a bridge connecting two different themes or events or even styles. You can write about the way they are connected or simply indicate a change with the use of a blank space. In her extraordinary memoir, *Memorial Drive*, Natasha Trethewey shifts both voice and tone, writing as "I" ("I have come into the room and am standing in front of the door . . .") in Chapter 5, and shifting to the paradoxically more intimate "you" in Chapter 6 ("You remember even though you don't want to . . ."), using only the blank space between chapters as a bridge. It works very well, better than any attempt to explain the shift could ever do.

How do you know what will work and what will not? Like so much else in life, in the end the only way to know what works is to try it out.

Transitions can be especially challenging when you are forging new ideas and making unconventional connections along the way.

One way to carry the reader to a new territory is through an image. (The more abstract your idea is, the more it will benefit from a concrete example.) Like sound, images weave together subjects not usually connected through sensual experience. They allow the reader to make a leap because the landing appears familiar, like solid ground.

Sometimes you will need more than one transition, if for example you are following both a story and a train of thought. Including two transitions, even if one seems like a stage whisper, facilitates perception. Perhaps because a weave is usually made of more than one thread.

Transitions can also give you unexpected insights, revelations that will lead eventually to a deeper understanding of your work. By connecting different elements, even if only by using space to indicate a change, you are creating a whole from the various parts you have written. And as readers navigate the bridges you've built, they will be discovering the whole terrain too. Bit by bit, bridge by bridge, a clear vision arises. Which is why, as you consider what bridge to build and how to do it, once again, taking a walk or even sleeping on the question is a good idea. Knowledge takes time to ripen.

Juxtapositions

Juxtaposition engages the imagination of your audience so that they can fill in the gaps. In film this technique is known as montage. In its literal sense, montage simply denotes editing. But this word also stands for a method of editing in which you put one thing next to another without explaining the connection. If you have seen the classic 1925 Eisenstein film *Battleship Potemkin*, you will not have forgotten the classic series of shots: one of various people on an outdoor staircase, including a very old woman and a younger woman pushing a pram that holds an infant, the next of the battleship in the harbor below, and the next of the old woman, her glasses shattered, screaming, followed by a shot of the pram rolling by itself down the stairs. If you are in the audience, you put two and two together while coming to the conclusion, almost without thinking, that the battleship has fired into the crowd on the staircase.

A similar effect can be used in literature. In my book *Woman and Nature*, in which each section is made up of several short pieces, I juxtapose a piece called "Mules" with one called "Show Horses." I don't spell out the connection, which is that women are pressed into both roles, roles that are demeaning while also contradictory. Even as I write these words, to spell out the connection in this way feels like an oversimplification. Instead, by allowing the reader to come to this and other conclusions, the meaning is allowed to become more nuanced and even open ended. And finally, enlisting the reader as a collaborator is both democratic and creative, allowing as it does the insight to continue developing in the minds and hearts of others.

Such an instance occurred while Eisenstein and Tisse were in the Crimea shooting the scenes on the Cruiser Potemkin. One day they went south from Sevastopol . . . and came to Alupka, once a palace of the Tsars of Russia. Walking around the formal garden, they saw the marble lions decorating the flight of steps leading from the palace to the lower garden. The first lion lay asleep. The second lion had awakened. The third was rising. Montage!

Three pieces of film recording could be edited to cause a stone lion to move!

—MARIE SETON, *Sergei M. Eisenstein*

Power Points

First lines and last lines are by their nature auspicious. Whether they begin a work, a chapter, a passage, or a paragraph, they act like what some practitioners of acupuncture call *power points*. There are points where it can be healing to insert needles all over the body, but they are not all equal. Some have a more powerful effect than others. The first lines and last lines of any piece of writing are power points. First lines draw you into a new world, one that at first you may not even be able to name, but you enter willingly because you are curious, or moved, or pleased, or surprised, or motivated in some other way you cannot yet name.

First lines can catch you off guard, as does "Viciousness in the kitchen!" Daring you to read more, the first line of Sylvia Plath's poem "Lesbos" takes you immediately into an intense world of forbidden feelings. The last line may not be a summation but it must be a destination. What has come before has been a journey during which both the writer and reader have experienced some change. Plath's poem ends with the line "Even in your Zen heaven we shan't meet," claiming the anger and hostility that, in the beginning, the speaker had projected onto the kitchen.

Poetic Progression

One way that the structure of any work can evolve is through poetry. Poetry is another country. If an accurate map of the arts were to be drawn, verse would border on music and dance. Indeed, poems are a form of music, one made from words.

In our shared past, the line between literature and music was far less definitive than it is now. Before written language was in use, epic poems were memorized and spoken and, in this way, passed down from one generation to the next. In the course of this development, various narratives were shaped by sound as much as content.

Listen to the lines (from a wonderful translation by Caroline Alexander) that open Book 7 of the *Iliad*:

> As god grants to yearning sailors
> a fair wind, when they labor at their well worn oars
> flogging the sea, and their limbs with fatigue are
> weak beneath them,
> so now the two appeared to the yearning Trojans.

Not only in poetry but in poetic or musical prose, repeated syllables and words, the rhythms of lines (called meter), the repetition of consonants (called alliterations) as in *god grants*, and the sonorous echoes of vowels, all seasoned with slight variations, create music.

Both poems and poetic prose convey meaning but they also speak from another realm of consciousness, a creative, sometimes cryptic way of knowing and being. A form of consciousness that is awakened by all music, kindred to reveries and dreams, intuition, along with supposedly sudden insights (that somehow you may suspect you have known for a long time), and the kind of revelation that you feel in your bones.

Listen to these lines from a poem by June Jordan, "In Memoriam: Martin Luther King, Jr."

> tomorrow yesterday rip rape
> exacerbate despoil disfigure
> crazy running threat the
> deadly thrall
> appall belief dispel

If a kind of magic occurs within these lines that carries the reader right to the heart of the matter, the same magic doubtless carried the writer as she wrote, fueling a direction and building the structure of the poem.

The music of the words you write can beckon and move you into the depths of yourself, to retrieve what you have perceived but haven't allowed yourself to know before, except perhaps in dreams.

And there is this too. Neuroscientist Indre Viskontas tells us that the same center in the brain that is connected to our muscles is also connected to the voice box. Accordingly, you just may need to dance to find your way as you write.

Thought, meaning, vision, the very words come after the music has been established and in the most mysterious way, they're already contained within it.

—C. K. WILLIAMS, *On Whitman*

(How I Learned to Write)

Several years before I entered high school, as the music of all that I read incited an alchemy that occurred almost involuntarily in my mind, I started writing poetry and short stories. Like most of those that I favored, my poems did not rhyme. The absence of any strict literary form mirrored a rebellion from social formalities that, especially in the repressive decade of the fifties, flourished among the young. (At the time, I hardly grasped that free verse *was* a form and that I had adopted it.)

The absence of rhyme was not the only trait of modern poetry that inspired me. I remember feeling what seemed almost like an electric shock when I encountered the first lines of a poem by Arthur Rimbaud: "And so the Mother, shutting up the duty book, / Went, proud and satisfied. She did not see the look / In the blue eyes, or how with secret loathing wild, / Beneath the prominent brow, a soul raged in her child . . ." It would be years before I realized that I was standing in a long line of writers, Allen Ginsberg and Patti Smith among them, who also felt liberated by Rimbaud's poetry. The brutal honesty of his voice cleared a path through the stiflingly conventional atmosphere of those times. To quote a line from his epic, *The Drunken Boat*, "the waters let me go my own free way."

Silent Spaces

The empty spaces that stand for silence, which you find between paragraphs or longer passages, play a crucial role in literature.

Just as it does in music, from the very small pauses between words to the slightly longer pauses between sentences to the cessation of sound that at times seems to reverberate at the end of a speech, silence is a pivotal element whether in language or in the structure of any given work.

In both music and language, silence is indispensable to any rhythmic pattern. Without silence, all you would hear, whether in a song, a tap dance, the clapping that accompanies flamenco, a poem, or even an ordinary sentence, is one uninterrupted and eventually intrusive sound.

The empty space around a text can also act like a frame, calling the reader's attention to what is written inside.

But silent as it is, this space is not passive. Required for prayer and meditation, sought by saints and pilgrims, silence is the home ground of contemplation. It's the equivalent of drawing breath. Take a breath and think about what you've just read, an empty space says to the reader.

The philosopher Ludwig Wittgenstein began his famous *Blue Book* with a single sentence:

"What is the meaning of a word?"

In isolating this question from the rest of the text, he draws the reader's attention to it and induces, even if momentarily, a thoughtful curiosity. To begin with a question, followed by silence, is often used as a pedagogical tool, and for good reason. It invites an attempt at an answer.

In his "Lecture on Nothing" John Cage creates a playful

landscape of sound and silence, while revealing a paradox within silence.

> I am here   . and there is nothing to say   .
> if among you are
> those who wish to get   somewhere . let them leave at
> any moment .   what we require   is
> silence   ;   but what silence requires
>   is   that I go on talking   .

Since silence is the cessation of sound, it is both defined and framed by sound.

Or you might say that silence and sound are dancing together.

Listen to the way silence matches steps with sound in this refrain in Ray Noble's lyrics for the 1930s song "The Very Thought of You":

> The very thought of you
> And I forget to do
> The little ordinary things
> That ev'ryone ought to do.

The pauses that are implied by the line breaks above are aesthetically pleasing. But they have another purpose too. They provide space and time for an emotional response to the lyrics. You think of someone you love (pause). You find yourself forgetting (pause). You realize just how (pause) disoriented, or indeed in love, you are. Each emotion that is evoked resonates in the silences between these lines.

To invoke another paradox, whenever you are the writer, you

will also be a reader. Indeed, the first reader. So as you read what you have written, listen for the silences. And if what you've written feels ponderous, hard to follow, heavy, or cramped, instead of adding more words, perhaps you need to add more silent spaces. In this sense, a text should be more like a living room than a storage space, a room through which you can walk easily or, unencumbered by the presence of too many things, a place where you can sit and gaze out at the view.

It is important that the ancient languages should be taught in schools today because they reveal the origins of language in silence, the power of silence over language, and the healing influence of silence on language so much more clearly than these things are revealed today in our own language.

It is also important that through the ancient languages that are "useless," man should be redeemed from the world of mere profit and utility.

—MAX PICARD, *The World of Silence*

And Then . . .

> There's the scarlet thread of murder running through the colorless skein of life, and our duty is to unravel it and isolate it and expose every inch of it.
>
> —SHERLOCK HOLMES IN ARTHUR
> CONAN DOYLE, *A Study in Scarlet*

As you are structuring a sentence, you might want to follow the chronology of the events. For example, instead of "She knocked on the front door, after parking her car," you may well decide that the following sentence sounds much better: "After parking her car, she knocked on the front door." Now you have a small narrative, a sequence of events, rather than an isolated action appended by a distracting afterthought.

Chronologies can be used in many ways, to structure paragraphs as well as sentences, passages, chapters, or whole books, as with memoirs, historical accounts, fictional work, and perhaps especially detective stories. Along with the question, "What will come next?" a chronology inherently carries a measure of suspense. Will the front door be answered? Who will answer it? Will our heroine be invited inside?

A chronological order can animate a scene, as it does in this passage from Virginia Woolf's novel, *Mrs. Dalloway*:

> The car had gone, but it left a slight ripple which flowed through glove shops and hat shops and tailors' shops on both sides of Bond Street. For thirty seconds all heads were inclined the same way—to the window.

In Woolf's description, as someone notable passes by, the psychological effect of rank and fame on a crowd becomes not only visible but an event in itself.

A chronological order does not have to move forward in time. It can also move backward. A famous example of a flashback frames all seven volumes of Marcel Proust's *In Search of Lost Time* as the narrator begins to remember his childhood. Chronology can be used to depict consciousness in many different directions. Ten years after the publication of the first volume of Proust's masterpiece, *Swann's Way*, T. S. Eliot, in *The Waste Land*, his great poem written after World War I, looks into a future that holds disturbing memories from the past:

> There is a shadow under this red rock,
> (Come in under the shadow of this red rock),
> And I will show you something different from either
> Your shadow at morning striding beside you
> Or your shadow at evening rising to meet you;
> I will show you fear in a handful of dust.

Whether depicting three dimensional events or the development of thought, though it can be slippery if not unnerving in real life, chronology is usually reliable as a way to order whatever you write.

In this regard, the classic detective story, which trades in frightening events, often murders, can also be comforting in the end. Although the detective story is driven by terrifying crimes, the chronology of the narrative is shaped by the logical deductions of a detective while asking who did what to whom and *when*. Chronology here does not simply order an inexorable chain of events, but also provides a key to identifying the guilty party and in this way confirms the rule of law, ensuring public safety once more.

Detectives of course come in many forms. Both Freud and Einstein solved mysteries, one about the nature of the human psyche and the other about the physical nature of the universe, and in writing about their insights, as they explained the conclusions for which they are now famous, they often ordered their explanations by portraying the development of their ideas chronologically.

If you are flying without a plan as you write sentences and then paragraphs, the work itself should reveal bits and pieces and finally all of the plan that is intrinsic to the work. It's there—you just have to be patient and listen for it, the way Miss Marple watches and listens again and again in novels by her creator, Agatha Christie—who, by the way, did not always know who committed the murder as she started each mystery, but instead, like her very observant detectives, often discovered the shape of the plot as she worked.

A deep motive for making literature or art of any sort is the desire to defeat the formlessness of the world and cheer oneself up by constructing forms out of what might otherwise seem a mass of senseless rubble.

—IRIS MURDOCH, *Existentialists and Mystics: Writings on Philosophy and Literature*

And Thus

As readers, most of us know that concrete examples or stories make abstract ideas far easier to grasp. But far less understood is the need to frame stories, novels, and memoirs with developing ideas. *And then* should be shadowed by *and thus*. A good example of this is, again, the detective story, in which every detail, from the shade of lipstick a woman wears, to the kind of car her niece drives, to the stain on the cuff of a young man's shirt is framed by a continuing inquiry and its contingent ideas concerning why this or that person is a suspect.

To cite a more subtle example, *What You Have Heard Is True*, Carolyn Forché's account of a famous and harrowing journey to Salvador that she took over three decades ago, is threaded with a continuing question, one that gradually develops from *why did her guide invite her on this journey*, to *what did he want to teach her*, to, by implication, *how did the conditions she witnessed come to pass*, and finally to *what was she supposed to do with what she learned*? A question that in the end, and silently, the book leaves each reader to answer too.

As a writer, you are in essence interrogating your experience. Though the style you use to articulate themes, questions, and causations may vary from heavy and didactic to barely detectible, depending on what is in fashion and your inclinations, reflection should be present in some form, even when, if not spoken directly, a theory or insight is implied by the order in which you arrange sentences, paragraphs, and passages.

And speaking of subtlety, here is another strange and inexplicable phenomenon many writers have experienced: At times, when you have a sufficiently clear idea of the forces behind what you describe, that understanding will end up between the lines, and your readers will somehow take it in even when you don't spell it out in any evident way.

In a certain sense, all writing or perhaps all good writing is driven by a search for meaning. But in this regard, you need not, as with scientific inquiry, come to a hard and fast conclusion. Indeed, despite how common it is and the difficulty it causes in our lives, ambiguity in literature is highly valued.

All novels, because they move repeatedly between action and reflection, are simultaneously about private experience and public events.

—JANE SMILEY, *13 Ways of Looking at the Novel*

Symmetry and Asymmetry

> Why, you might just as well say that "I see what I eat" is the same thing as "I eat what I see"!
> —THE MAD HATTER IN LEWIS CARROLL'S
> *Alice in Wonderland*

Symmetrical patterns of speech can be used very effectively to highlight differences. In an essay on dance, Clair Wills writes about the difficulty of describing "what it feels like as opposed to what it looks like." The repetition of "it" and "like" makes the contrast more dramatic.

Kimberlé Crenshaw does something similar to even greater effect when she argues that "Treating different things the same can generate as much inequality as treating the same things differently."

In each case, an asymmetry is couched within a verbal symmetry. The similarity in syntax highlights the asymmetry in meaning.

There is something inherently satisfying in these paradoxical constructions, as when the March Hare argues in Lewis Carroll's *Alice in Wonderland* that "I like what I get" is hardly the same as "I get what I like." By such paradoxical logic we are thrust into a puzzle, one whose solution often leads us to better understand the hidden side of whatever has captured our gaze.

A Sense of Proportion

It may not always be evident but often it is. Ask yourself what is central to your work versus what is a minor aspect or even a digression. Then allot the space—which in the reader's experience is time—or number of words you assign to any given subject, incident, or character accordingly. Regarding such arrangements, this is one way a novel differs from a short story. The former, being far more capacious, can host a number of digressions. Readers in the nineteenth century had a greater tolerance for these, as you will be able to observe if you read Hugo, Balzac, or Melville. These writers were composing on a larger canvas than is common today, one that included a wide variety of subjects, from social conditions and histories, to manners and gastronomy, to the physiology of whales. In contemporary work these elements are often implied though not elaborated. But whatever your practice is, pay attention to proportion. It is somehow confusing if not disturbing when too much space is given to a tangential issue—like a small house with a very large garage.

Lists

If you are overwhelmed with all you want to describe or include in what you are writing, try compiling a list.

You will find lists in much of the oldest literature we have. In the *Iliad*, to cite a famous example, Homer lists all the fine Athenian ships that are waiting in the harbor for the wind to rise so that they can sail to Troy, where they will wage war. Epic poems usually contain more than one list. This was a way to preserve history in a recitation of names and as such was also a mnemonic device. The list would be passed on orally, often by singing it, to each generation. But serving collective memory was not the list's only use. Lists exist in many cultures as part of the liturgies that accompany rituals too. They do more than contain information; they are incantations, putting both singer and worshipper in a trance through which a higher order of knowledge becomes accessible. (This is what happens with Tibetan Buddhist as well as Catholic chants, to name just two examples.)

Something of that older purpose remains in the secular literature that followed. In Shakespeare's Sonnet #116, he lists the qualities of true love, as in an "ever-fixed mark" and "the star to every wand'ring bark," or "not Time's Fool," endowing romantic love with cosmic dimensions. A few centuries later, in *Leaves of Grass*, Walt Whitman carves a sacred experience out of practical work using the resonance of a list, "I Hear America Singing":

> . . . the varied carols I hear,
> Those of mechanics, each one singing his as it should
> be blithe and strong,

The carpenter singing his as he measures his plank or
   beam,
The mason singing his as he makes ready for work . . .

And here's a list, from Rilke's *The Book of Hours*, that gives material shape to the poet's feelings while at the same time conveying their source in mystical experience:

You, the great homesickness we could never shake off,
you, the forest that always surrounded us,
you, the song we sang in every silence,
you dark net threading through us.
(TRANS. ANITA BARROWS AND JOANNA MACY)

The enchanting effect of lists can perhaps be attributed to the magic of language itself. Small children like to say the names of people, places, and things they love, as if in that way they can keep them close. By naming we are also summoning and thus conquering through sound the troubling nature of absence. This is what the shaman, priest, rabbi, and imam do, even when they are calling angels. But it's also what writers do. We summon or more properly evoke worlds with lists.

And out of these lists we can also create new visions not by argument but through a resonance that forges connections not usually made. In a contemporary work, poet David Shaddock's "In This Place Where Something's Missing Lives" lists paired atrocities, one inflicted in Vietnam, another suffered by a protestor in America: "The white phosphorous bombs / The bone seeking fire. / The rubber bullets and swinging batons / the train wheels cutting a man's legs." Of course if you know the history you know the man who lost his legs was protesting against the Vietnam War. So intellectually that connection is not new. But what Shaddock does here is forge an emotional connection through the evocation of the brutality that shaped both.

Finally, lists can be lighthearted too, even humorous. Reading Donald Hall's memoir, *A Carnival of Losses: Notes on Nearing Ninety*, you find a short list in his description of the caftans he remembers his mother wearing: "It reached from her shoulders to the floor, was easy to put on and take off, and required no underwear."

Repetition

The difference between the kind of repetition you ought to avoid and the kind that you choose to include and foster is delicate. In general the first is unintended and the second desired.

Bearing this in mind, the difference between intended and untended repetition can be compared to the difference between dancing and stumbling across a room. And like dancing, repetition when it is intended has rhythm, a not inconsequential aspect of literature.

When it's done on purpose, to repeat phrases is kindred to listing, since the names of things, places, and beings in a list are often accompanied by repeated phrases.

Listen, for instance, to this Apache ceremonial song for masked dancers:

> When my songs first were, they made my songs with
> words of jet.
> Earth when it was made
> Sky when it was made
> Earth to the end
> Sky to the end . . .

Here the repeated phrases "it was made" and "to the end" have been added to the list.

This gives the list both unity and rhythm, the power that comes from any sound that is repeated, whether it be a voice thick with pleasure repeating the name of a lover or a deceptively complicated but irresistibly repetitive drumbeat.

And like a drumbeat, repetition can convey many different

tones and meanings. Take for instance a disturbing passage from Virginia Woolf's novel, *Mrs. Dalloway*, when Septimus, a young man suffering shell shock, responds to his doctor's orders that he must separate himself from the woman he loves:

> "Must," "must," why "must"? What power had Bradshaw over him?
> "What right did Bradshaw have to say 'must' to me?" he demanded.

In such an expression of anger, repetition seems almost organic, the resonance of an emotion.

But repetition often plays still another role. Like the stitching in a garment, to repeat a phrase or sentence can provide the structure for the whole work. The song of the masked dancers, for instance, begins with these lines:

> When the earth was made
> when the sky was made
> when my songs were first heard.

The sense of an integrated whole is often achieved through formal structures that dictate rhythm and also rhyme. Many literary forms call for repetitions, most notably the villanelle and the pantoum, poetic forms that require repeating lines in particular positions. In this way, the poet is not only repeating lines within the poem, but repeating a form that many writers before have used, continuing an echo through time.

A similar but different effect can be summoned by the chorus in a drama, which often describes dramatic action that has just taken place on stage, implying an echo through the larger social body that bears witness and may even be suffering the consequences of the same tragic events.

Repetition in the form of a ritual or ceremony that is itself repeated, as with Christian ritual every Sunday, is an integral part of most religious practices. As Unitarian minister and writer Marilyn Sewell has said, repetition yields a sense of a predictable order that, especially in times of crisis, either personal or public, can be comforting.

Rhyme is another kind of repetition, tying words with different meanings together through echoing sounds, placing often unruly emotions, such as passionate love, in a larger musical landscape.

Demanding literary forms also offer writers the solace of a predictable order in the wilderness of creation. Though one of these forms, the sonnet, requires a disruption, what is called a *volta*, meaning *turn*, by which the meaning in the preceding verses is often turned on its head or at least in an unexpected direction.

In both poetry and prose, repetition creates rhythm and rhythm cradles consciousness. This can be a magical process in which, as Whitman writes in "Out of the Cradle Endlessly Rocking," past, present, and future fuse ("uniter of here and hereafter"), while a grown man can shed the tears of "a little boy again."

In a novel or a story the rhythm of repetition can often be found in the structure. In *If on a Winter's Night a Traveler*, Italo Calvino repeatedly turns to address the reader directly about the act of reading, beginning in the first chapter with the first line, "You are about to begin reading Italo Calvino's new novel . . ." commencing the second chapter with "you have now read about thirty pages and you're becoming caught up in the story . . ." proceeding in the next to "an odor of frying wafts at the opening of the page" and so on, regularly breaking the fourth wall by speaking to the reader about the process of writing and reading. This would hardly have the same effect if he did it only once. Repeated, it not only establishes a style, but draws the parameters of an intimate relationship with the reader. And in the end the structure of the book will weave the many disparate tales into one story, which is, of course, about readers.

As with fabric, whether in poetry or prose, the tensile strength of the work depends on each thread of meaning being woven throughout the work. The trick is to repeat without seeming repetitious. But if you aim for an evolution of the meaning, you will accomplish that.

Weight-Bearing Symbols

Sometimes unity is created in a paragraph, a passage, or even a whole work through the use of a metaphor. A paragraph in Elaine Sciolino's book about the river Seine, for example, begins by suggesting that after exploring the river, to walk west along the river toward the Eiffel Tower would provide "a perfect climax." At the end of this paragraph, she extends this metaphor in a subtle way by describing Paris and the Seine as lovers.

A metaphor can also be used to insert a second narrative within a larger plotline. In his novel *The Secret Agent*, Joseph Conrad uses the image of a tightrope to portray the emotional state of one of his characters, the Chief Inspector, while he is dealing with the disapproval of an Assistant Commissioner: "He felt at the moment like a tight-rope artist might feel if suddenly, in the middle of the performance, the manager of the Music Hall were to rush out . . . and begin to shake the rope." Several pages later in the same scene, Conrad writes, "The indignation of a betrayed tight-rope performer was strong within him. In his pride of a trusted servant he was affected by the assurance that the rope was not shaken for the purpose of breaking his neck . . ."

Two sentences later, as the quietly threatening exchange continues, he extends the metaphor by writing, "He was not afraid of getting a broken neck." In the next paragraph, depicting the Assistant Commissioner, Conrad writes that "His manner was easy and businesslike while he persisted in administering another shake to the tight rope." And after continuing what is proving to be a precipitous dialogue, Conrad explains that the Chief Inspector decided to "jump off the rope," extending the metaphor even further by telling us that he "came to the ground with gloomy frankness."

The tightrope here lends the passage a second line of suspense, at the same time as it provides an emotional structure to a scene in which, underneath the evident content concerning the investigation of a crime, is a treacherous struggle between two men, one of whom holds more power than the other.

And I detect still another metaphor at work here, which is that the power struggles in the government, between officials, mirrors the power struggle between classes and ideologies that motivated the terrorist act of violence at the heart of the novel.

Metaphors can be beautiful or startling or clever, memorable or almost too subtle to detect, but when they are part of the structure of the work, what is most important is that they are up to the job. To use the metaphor implied in the term "structure," they act like columns that are not just decorative but must be strong enough to bear the weight they carry.

The best metaphors are usually close by. The Seine, for instance, is a site where lovers often meet. And regarding *The Secret Agent*, walking on a tightrope was an act commonly performed in London's music halls, venues that sailors frequented, familiar to Conrad, a sailor for two decades (and where, earlier in the novel, Conrad sets a meeting between two anarchists).

Speaking of the familiar, no wonder indeed that metaphors are so effective in providing structure to literature. They structure our minds too. We think through associations. We like whatever we encounter to rhyme as well as reason. This is why some contemporary thinkers believe our picture of a world in which one thing is connected to another is illusory. But others believe that our minds mirror nature, and that it really is all connected.

The perfect climax is a walk west along the river toward the Eiffel Tower, the most distinctive emblem of Paris . . . Without the Eiffel Tower, Paris would still exist; without the Seine, there never would have been a Paris. While the river owes the city its romantic aura, the city owes the river its birth, its life, and its identity. The love affair of Paris and the Seine defines them both.

—ELAINE SCIOLINO,
The Seine: The River That Made Paris

Sticking the Landing

If you've ever watched young gymnasts compete, you know what sticking the landing means. After astonishing feats on the bars, these athletes fly off into the air and land, one hopes squarely on two feet, with both hands raised up, signaling successful completion. You can stick the landing when you write too.

Along with the end of a work, the end of a passage, a chapter, or a paragraph is a power point. It completes whatever has gone before, at times reaching a logical conclusion, whether of an event or an argument, sometimes echoing your first sentence but with changes that reflect what the preceding paragraph has revealed, sometimes opening a new dimension. Sometimes capturing the essence of a tragedy, at others concluding with what seems like a swift jolt of wit.

I mention these categories to give you some examples. But this should not be considered an exhaustive catalogue. There are as many strong endings as there are stories to tell. The point is to be aware of what is a necessity but also an opportunity. The last line of a paragraph provides a moment of drama, during which your reader can cry or laugh or nod in strong agreement with you.

How do you do it? I imagine it's the same with those gymnasts, a mixture of craft, practice, and an unwavering concentration on the task at hand. As you write the paragraph, listen to it carefully, and let the combination of sound and meaning carry you to what will seem the best if not an inevitable conclusion, a sturdy landing, two feet on the ground.

The Historian cannot capture a process so slow as the death of a marriage. He would need some other medium than the pen to do it with—perhaps one of those cameras that photograph the growing of a plant and the unfolding of its blossoms. With such a camera we could see the expressions change, telescoping the imperceptible changes of seven years into a few moments. We watch the passionate adoring glances glaze to cordiality, grow expressionless, contract with pain. The once ardent glances are now averted: fingers disentwine and are folded behind the separate backs. Backs are turned.

—DIANE JOHNSON, *The True History of the First Mrs. Meredith and Other Lesser Lives*

Telling Stories

Telling Stories

The human capacity for language and storytelling
go hand in hand.

—LESLIE MARMON SILKO, *Storyteller*

It makes sense that, as Leslie Marmon Silko writes, language would have evolved as a means to tell stories. No one knows for certain how early in human history we began to tell stories. The urge to create a narrative seems fundamental to human nature. Handed down from one generation to the next, the tales we tell have transmitted history, genealogies, and shared values, telling us where and who we are. Even when we are asleep, we tell stories in our dreams.

Of course, storytelling is central to fiction. But stories play an essential role in essays too. A story is not just a literary form—it is a mode of thought. Einstein explored his theory of relativity by imagining a very short story in which a stationary witness sees two lightning bolts strike both ends of a speeding train simultaneously, a witness who makes measurements indicating, erroneously, that the bolts struck each end of the train at different times. When a concept is illustrated by a concrete example, it is far easier for the reader to understand. But the writer benefits too. Einstein used stories not only to illustrate his theories but to develop his ideas.

The best stories do not tell you what you ought to feel but instead recreate events that evoke emotion. After reading an essay by Emma Goldman, you might agree that it is unfair that women have no rights over their own children. But reading Tolstoy's *Anna Karenina*, you can feel the misery that occurs as a consequence of this injustice.

As Freud realized when he invented what he called "talk therapy," by telling stories, we discover and even heal ourselves. A powerful story even has the capacity to change the very structure of the psyche. Indeed, the way we live our lives is inextricably linked to all the stories we have been told and tell ourselves.

When we listen to a story, our brains experience the action as if it were happening to us. Brain scanning studies show that when we hear about characters emoting, the emotional areas of our brains become active; when we hear about characters moving vigorously, the motor regions of our brains are roused.

—ANNIE MURPHY PAUL, *The Extended Mind*

(How I Learned to Write)

It's no coincidence that soon after I entered high school, I began to be able to tell the full story of my childhood. It was perhaps because my best friend, I'll call her Cathy, had not just one but two parents who were alcoholics, a fact she did nothing to hide. That's one reason why I trusted her so much. We had been drinking a great deal ourselves one night when I began to cry uncontrollably. What exactly triggered my confession I do not know—though I'm certain that alcohol played a role. I found myself telling her how when my mother returned very drunk from a night of barhopping, or when she had been drinking by herself at home, she would begin to attack me verbally, as if I were a sworn enemy she had to cut down with her words. By then I had ceased to hide the fact of her drinking, but clearly on a less than conscious level I had taken her bitter cascade of recriminations to heart. Which is why I never spoke of it. Until I told Cathy. I have no doubt now that this confession enabled me in my writing. Telling that story allowed me to tell many others. And just as important, to listen closely to the stories that others tell.

Forbidden Ground

There is so much unwritten that needs to be written.
——TILLIE OLSEN, *Silences*

Various kinds of censorship conspire against us as we write. Often the forbidden knowledge is generally known but simply not talked about in "polite society." I am thinking of a passage near the end of Virginia Woolf's *Mrs. Dalloway* when Clarissa Dalloway, disturbed about what one of her guests told her, has left her party for a few moments to collect herself. Dr. Bradshaw had just described a terrible incident, one that happened earlier in the day, the suicide of a young man. "What business had the Bradshaws to talk of death at her party?" Clarissa asks herself, outraged, as despite herself she imagines this death. "Her body went through it first," Woolf writes.

The open secret depicted here concerned the emotional damage sustained by a generation of young men during the First World War, which led to the high rate of suicide among them.

Other secrets may be common knowledge within a limited group, a family, a business, a circle of friends. When everyone knows, for instance, that a father or an uncle or a cousin is an alcoholic, yet that word is never spoken.

Perhaps because we are storytelling creatures, unwritten censorship can cause extensive damage. If, as Ursula Le Guin writes, "Storytelling is a tool for knowing who we are and what we want," by the same measure, silencing a story prevents us from knowing ourselves and, like an impermeable barrier in the mind, can impede writing altogether.

What remains unspoken takes residence inside, inhabiting the body, immobile, terrified, and mute, replaced on the outside with what seems vague and trivial by comparison.

No wonder then that great writing so often breaks silences, whether private or collective. Though for years it was something that, along with countless other women, I experienced every month, I remember clearly the elation I felt the first time I found anything in literature that depicted a woman menstruating. The book is called *The Golden Notebook* and within its pages, Doris Lessing describes a scene in which her heroine is disturbed by the stain and smell of her menses. Yet despite her character's repulsion, the inclusion of menstruation in this account of a woman's life was thrilling to generations of women who had been taught to treat our monthly cycles as something that should be hidden.

Physical experience, sexuality, pleasure, homosexuality, affairs and pregnancies outside marriage, "illegitimate" children, masturbation, menstruation, rape, molestation, sexual abuse whether of men or women or children, emotional abuse, "wife beating," unhappiness in marriage, racism and the violence of racism—all these experiences have been subject to a polite silence. And they have all been subjects of extraordinary literature.

When you find yourself falling silent as you write about any subject, ask yourself if there is some secret you are afraid to reveal or a silence you hesitate to break.

It's a fearsome process, treading on forbidden ground. But, in the arc of justice, worth the effort many times over. As is written in the Gospel of Thomas, "If you bring forth what is within you, what you bring forth will save you. If you do not bring forth what is within you, what you do not bring forth will destroy you."

Histories

When did the story you're telling occur? No matter when it was, even if it's fiction, it must have a place in history. (Unless it's science fiction—and then at least a place in invented history.) Thus, while telling a story, if it's your memory or an event from another life or an invented character's life, you can always turn to the surrounding history for inspiration. Are you describing an event from the sixties? Would the election of JFK, the Cuban Missile Crisis, JFK's assassination, or the assassination of Martin Luther King Jr. resonate in any way with the family argument you are writing about? An event from history could lead you to understand a dimension of the story you're telling that you had not observed before. While writing one of my own books, I came to understand the alcoholism on the Irish side of my family as an effect of the colonization of Ireland by Great Britain. But the connection can be far more subtle, even if it's just an atmosphere of hope mixed with divisiveness and violence you sense in the mood of the times in which your story takes place.

Research

Very often, what you are writing requires research. This can be true for fiction as well as nonfiction. If you have set your love story in early nineteenth-century France, for instance, at the very least you will most probably need to know what men and women of all classes habitually wore and how they styled their hair. Even if you were alive during the period in which you set your narrative, there will be events you don't remember clearly or aspects for which you lack precise details. So by one means or another, you'll have to hunt them down.

Often writers choose, if possible, to observe a place or an event or to talk to witnesses directly. Victor Hugo acquired his knowledge of prison life, which he portrays in *Les Misérables,* during a visit to the notorious Bagne de Toulon, where men who had been sentenced to row the galleys of France's Mediterranean fleet or to work in the local shipyards were housed.

If Hugo were aiming to write a doctoral thesis on conditions at this prison, he would have felt compelled to be methodical, citing the most respected references to support his observations, including official reports and interviews with bureaucrats, guards, and prisoners. But *Les Misérables* is a novel, not an academic work. Though he may have used some official studies or documents, to make the experience of prisoners in this formidable prison come alive, Hugo relied on what he observed himself, and the empathy he felt.

In literature, research is not presented as proof of an argument but rather integrated into the vision of reality the book creates (this applies to both fiction and nonfiction). Hugo folds what he learned about this particular prison into his narrative in bits and pieces here and there, as in an early scene between Jean Valjean and

Bishop Myriel, the kind prelate who gives the ex-convict a meal and a bed for the night. Describing the prison from which he had so recently been freed, Hugo's hero Valjean tells the bishop ". . . the ball and chain at your feet, a plank to sleep on, the heat, the cold, hard galleys, the stick! Double shackles for nothing. The dungeon for a word. Even sick in bed, the chain. Dogs, dogs are better off!"

From this passage you can see that Hugo does not just put facts and figures on a page, but rather digests what he learned, so that Hugo's knowledge of the prison is spoken by Jean Valjean in a convincing way. Even when turned into a beautifully written, almost poetic speech, his description seems to emanate from the mouth of a man embittered by the nineteen years he served in prison.

When you are writing a creative work, you will need to take time to absorb and digest your research so that in some way it is your own.

There is always the possibility that what you learn in your research could cause you to change course, at times even proving you wrong about a conclusion or bias you held, yet at the same time it opens a window to a new vision of or direction for your work. It's a thin line you walk when you do research, between being loyal to your creative vision and receptive to new knowledge.

While you are searching, you may encounter surprises, some of which might well present a challenge to your preconceptions about your subject, even when, as in a memoir, you are writing about your own family. Though you may not want to reveal what you have learned, the work itself will eventually guide your choice. Does keeping the secret feel like you are telling a lie? Meanwhile the dilemma itself makes a moving story (a moving example of which can be found in Honor Moore's brilliant memoir, *The Bishop's Daughter.*)

Writers are always researching, or rather searching. (As James Baldwin has said, writing is a process of discovery.) Though this kind of searching may be less a conscious task than an orientation. No matter what you are doing, this search continues effortlessly every day and night. More than once in his notebooks, Henry James records words said in casual conversation by friends during a shared meal, comments that gave him subjects for stories or episodes in a novel.

Often a writer is not looking for answers to specific questions but simply wants to know more, to garner "a feel" for the subject. It's certainly possible to write about a place, for instance, without having ever been there. Franz Lehár set a famous scene in his opera, *The Merry Widow*, in Maxim's, without ever having been to that restaurant, or even Paris.

On the other hand, spending time in the places you are writing about can be invaluable. Crossing over the border between West and East Germany in the days before the Berlin Wall came down, driving on a dark one-lane country road outside Oakridge (where the first atom bomb was made) past a small, lone cabin as smoke rose from its chimney, or walking in the lab's institutional hallways, standing near ground zero in Hiroshima, or walking where so many barracks once stood in Dachau, I could feel the history these places held as if in my bones.

It's common for writers to conduct at least twice if not ten times the research that ends up on the page. Somehow what is never put into words is there. Between the lines, perhaps, or as the tone that grew out of what the author learned.

And there is this too: so many writers, in the end, despite having finished a work, continue their research in smaller ways, keeping the connection alive to what has become as much a part of them as their own memories.

The original objective when Ina and I moved to the edge of the Hill Country of Texas in 1978 was to learn about the boyhood and manhood of the young Lyndon Johnson. But while I was interviewing ranchers and farmers, and their wives, about him, I realized I was hearing, just in the general course of long conversations, about something else: what the lives of the women of the Hill Country had been like before, in the 1930s and '40s, the young congressman Lyndon Johnson brought electricity to that impoverished, remote, isolated part of America—how the lives of these women had, before "the lights" came, been lives of unending toil.

—ROBERT A. CARO, *Working*

Another Principle of Relativity

In literature as well as the physical world, countless different perspectives exist and they all provide effective ways to tell a tale.

Critics have noted that in the novels of Jane Austen, there are rarely, if ever, any scenes in which women are not present, speculating that Austen. herself would not have been privy to conversations held exclusively between men and thus did not try to depict these. At times a perspective represents a radical change, even a reversal, as in the Jean Rhys novel *Wide Sargasso Sea*, which tells the same story that Charlotte Brontë told in *Jane Eyre*, but from the point of view of Rochester's first wife, the one imprisoned upstairs, who is characterized in Brontë's novel as being insane.

Sometimes the perspective is less from the vantage point of a given person than from a preference or a value system. Simone Weil begins her famous essay, "The *Iliad*, or the Poem of Force," by declaring her perspective with the sentence, "The true hero, the real subject, the core of the *Iliad*, is might." The remainder of the essay convinces us of the truth of her assertion. Written during World War II, this essay expressed a slightly veiled resistance to the oppressive might of the Nazi armies that occupied France.

Your perspective is hardly ever universal. Rather, it is unique. But when you acknowledge your subjective view, perhaps because you are being forthright, paradoxically, your subjectivity creates a bond with the reader. Such honesty is not exactly the same as truth telling. It can be present even when the perspective is that of an unreliable narrator, as with Eudora Welty's "Why I Live at the

P.O." in which the narrator's complaints, however flawed, produce an accurate picture of what she is like.

Even if you chose to speak through an uninvolved, "objective" narrator, this perspective adds another dimension to the story you tell.

Reflection

> Painting is a way of reflecting on life—and reflection is more active than simple contemplation. It is the manifestation of a will to discern reality; to dig into it, to collaborate in its discovery and in its understanding. To paint is also to create reality.
> —ANTONI TÀPIES, *I am a Catalan*

Reflection includes more than the mirror image from which it takes its name. It adds a third element to the pair, the seer and the seen, and that is thought. With reflection you are not only seeing something and naming it, you are also thinking about it.

B. H. Fairchild's powerful poem, "Beauty," begins with a question posed by his wife as they stand in a museum in Florence. "What are you thinking?" she asks. "Beauty," he answers. What follows is a long and profound journey through memory, driven by a series of reflections on manhood and the constricting concepts of masculinity among the working men who occupied his life when he was a child, men with "muted passions," who never used or would use the word *beauty*.

To write requires an active kind of seeing in which not only do you see but you see yourself seeing and, as with the famous image within an image on a Quaker Oats box, you see yourself seeing yourself seeing too, all of which has consequences. Reflection not only requires light, it sheds light. No wonder then that writing is such a dynamic and at times unpredictable process. With each work, you learn as you go, while you read what you write and reflect on what you have written (a reflection that may change the direction of your thoughts).

In this way, you become present to yourself. A presence that is essential to writing. This sounds like a spiritual practice and in a way it is, but your goal is not self-improvement. It is only insight (and also, as a by-product of that, authenticity). So when Donald Hall describes an aspect of his grief after the death of his wife, Jane Kenyon, he is not contrite and has no plans to change his behavior when he writes, "When she was sick I slept surprisingly well. After she died I dreamt she left me for another man, and I went back to sleeping pills." And then he tells us that the pills worked better when he drank a glass of port just before taking them. Though this is surely not anything a self-help advocate would ever recommend, it makes for great writing. Not because it's strange behavior, but because so many of us have been there.

Thinking, existentially speaking, is a solitary but not a lonely business; solitude is that human situation in which I keep myself company. Loneliness comes about when I am alone without being able to . . . keep myself company, when as Jaspers used to say, "I am in default of myself."

—HANNAH ARENDT, *The Life of the Mind*

(How I Learned to Write)

My childhood did not fit with any conventional narrative. Beginning just after I turned five, following my parents' divorce, I was moved back and forth from my grandparents to my mother's home until finally, by the time I was thirteen years old, I ended up living with my father. Because he was a fireman who had to stay overnight at the station, I would often find myself alone at night, frightened as well as lonely. It was during this time, just after I entered high school, that I met a school friend's parents, Mort, who was a painter, and Gerry, an educator, specializing in dance. They were both admired by a group of new friends, who were aspiring artists and writers. We visited them frequently after school to talk about art. It was during one of those sessions that Gerry asked me if I'd like a job, helping her with meals and the children. Very soon they must have become aware of the precarity of my life because, bit by bit, they began to parent me. At first they might invite me to say overnight after babysitting. And then overnight stretched into long weekends, and at other times, every other night. Until one late afternoon, struck by a car as he was crossing the street, my father died. The night I was told of his death, I refused to go to my grandparents' house. Mort and Gerry took me in, soon becoming my legal guardians. I lived with them until the summer I graduated high school.

The house itself gave me an education of a kind. The pots Gerry used for cooking, the color of red earth, embellished with painted flowers, came from Mexico where they had lived for a few years. Mort's paintings of all the family, the kids, Josh and Carla, Gerry, hung on the walls. Even the architecture of the house, with Mort's glassed-in studio forming one wing, embodied a way of life, a life shaped by art, a way of living I studied as closely as any apprentice would.

A painting Mort did of me, shortly after my father's death, hangs in my living room today. A few weeks after my father died, Mort asked me if I might pose for him. He painted me in the morning, before breakfast, when I was still wearing the red striped men's flannel nightshirt I had found in our local Sears Roebuck. In the portrait my face has two distinct sides. I look sad and numb. But the side in shadow seems almost unconscious, as if I were immersed in the world of the dead, while the illuminated side seems to be quietly observing, perceptive. Altogether the painting is vibrant with resonant patterns, stripes on my nightshirt echoing the stripes on a small tablecloth behind me, contrasting planes of color, deep green, black balanced with swaths of white. As I've grown older, I've come to understand more and more the great gift he gave me, without compromising what he could see, creating a mirror that holds my loss and pain in beauty, the miracle artists and writers alike have learned to summon through the patterns of light and sound we can see and hear.

Interdependence

Resonance. I count all the time on resonance. I call on this, you see.

—JOSEF ALBERS INTERVIEWED BY
SEVIM FESCI, *Archives of American Art*

The Monterey pine that grows close to my house, but in my neighbor's yard, has no respect for private property. Dropping needles and pine cones on my side of the fence, it provides nests for birds that fly in from all directions and secret places for squirrels to hide the nuts they have found. The shade it offers will protect rhododendrons if I plant them near the fence but will not allow enough sunlight through to grow tomatoes or sunflowers under its branches. I am grateful for the tree I see every morning when I open the blinds, in more ways than one—not just because it cleans the air I breathe, but because it's part of the landscape of my consciousness, daily.

To recognize, understand, and work with the metrics of connection is a vital part of craft in every form of art. Bauhaus artist and teacher Josef Albers wrote a book called *Interaction of Color*, describing the way different colors affect one another when they are placed in proximity. He points out that we do not perceive colors near or next to each other separately but as part of a dynamic process through which what we see is altered by proximity, even creating what he calls "after images" in which patterns of colors are actually reversed and new colors appear.

A kind of aftereffect occurs in writing too. Once you include any sound or word (sentence, paragraph) in what you are writing, it will remain in the mind of the reader, even after several pages are turned.

The sounds of words are at least as dynamic as color if not more so. A syllable, whether pronounced or read, will persist in memory so that its influence continues through the words that follow. Listen to the way the sound indicated by the letter "s" repeats in the paragraph below, from James Joyce's famous short story "The Dead":

> The air of the room chilled his shoulders. He stretched himself cautiously along under the sheets and lay down beside his wife. One by one they were all becoming shades. Better to pass boldly into that other world, in the full glory of some passion, than fade and wither dismally with age.

You can almost hear the voice of the narrator whisper, coupled with an implied "hush" intended not to silence the storyteller but rather to invoke the silence that accompanies reverence.

Like the last movement of a symphony that at the end repeats a passage from the first movement, the last line of "The Dead" echoes the "s" in this paragraph, with greater intensity: "His soul swooned slowly, as he heard the snow falling faintly, like the descent of their last end, upon all the living and the dead."

When you place two words or sentences side by side, they will fuse in some way. Just as natural landscapes are filled with a variety of colors that blend in our perception, human emotions are neither singular nor monochromatic but almost always a mix of different, even contradictory responses.

When you tell any story, you create a system in which, as with a watershed, every word or sentence reflects and acts upon every other, in a way that, miraculous as it sometimes seems, is never static, but like nature is always evolving, transforming before your very eyes.

Foreshadowing

Foreshadowing provides a way of framing what is to come. Though it also follows the natural contours of the mind, the way we really think, which is rarely in strict chronological order.

A scene that is to happen later but is told earlier can be critical to a mystery, revealing clues that will build suspense, or even lure the reader toward the wrong suspect.

Or as in Patti Smith's superb memoir, *Just Kids*, foreshadowing can establish the real subject of what is to follow. Smith begins the foreword to her book with the words "I was asleep when he died" before describing how she prepared herself for the sad news that she knew would be coming, and the telephone call that delivered it.

However, the first chapter of the book, "Monday's Children" begins far back in time, when Smith was a child. Had the book begun with this chapter instead of the foreword, we might have thought it was simple autobiography. But it is not. It is an account of a profound friendship. Which we learn well before the book depicts the moment when the two friends first meet.

This is not at all confusing. It is in fact familiar. It follows a familiar narrative, the shape of mourning and of love.

I was asleep when he died. I had called the hospital to say one more good night, but he had gone under, beneath layers of morphine. I held the receiver and listened to his labored breathing through the phone, knowing I would never hear him again.

—PATTI SMITH, *Just Kids*

Being and Character

The best heroines and heroes seem as if they have grown from the inside. The details of how they look and dress, speak, or cross a room seem to fall into place naturally, while revealing who they are. The operative word here being *are*, a form, in fact, of *to be*.

The best description of how to depict a character I have ever heard came during an interview with an actor who had written a biography of Orson Welles, when he said he was surprised and happy to discover that writing is similar to acting in this regard: you have *to be* the character you are creating.

And of course, *being* is a verb. Like everything else on earth, who you are, what you know and do is always changing, and so it goes with characters too.

. . . Everything I have written, including the first book I wrote, even there, yes. Although I didn't know I was going to forever do it. Every one of those is a movement toward knowledge. And if somebody doesn't know—a main character—doesn't know something extremely important at the end of the book that he or she didn't know in the beginning or throughout, then it doesn't work for me. It's not like a happy ending. I don't mean that. It's just—and it's not an "Aha!" moment. It's just that you grow. You learn. Something, you know—

—TONI MORRISON IN AN INTERVIEW
WITH HILTON ALS IN *The New Yorker*,
AUGUST 7, 2019

Mysteries of the Soul

The process through which a book enters a writer's mind is usually embedded with meanings that will come to fruition as the tale is told. Speaking again of Michael Ondaatje's beautiful memoir, *Running in the Family*, he begins by revealing the process through which the book was engendered. Asleep during an icy winter in Ontario, he woke up covered in sweat and in tears. He had already planned a trip back to Ceylon, he tells us, because when he reached his mid-thirties, he realized that he had "slipped past a childhood," he had "ignored and not understood." This passage casts a pensive and wistful light over all that is to come, and with that a unique kind of suspense, the desire for answers that belong to the mysteries of the soul.

Invoking whatever is occurring in your process can also release you from whatever prohibitions may be haunting your efforts. If you are writing, for instance, about a family secret, you might begin by saying how uneasy it makes you to be telling it. Even if you delete this later, writing it down will act like an open sesame to the caves of forbidden memories we all carry inside.

Memories

Natasha Trethewey's deeply moving account of her mother's death, *Memorial Drive*, begins with her effort to retrieve her memories by visiting the scene of the crime. She drives past the gate to the apartment complex on Memorial Drive where her mother was murdered, "as if to remind me what is remembered here and what is not."

The shock suffered after a trauma can blunt memory, as if to protect the mind from the original shock. Stories heal but telling them often requires a sustained effort, as you slowly reassemble fragments, trying to recover a sense of the whole event from what has been shattered, a process that's present in the word: re-member.

Often, it's a single detail that helps to conjure the truth. While Trethewey stands under the window of the bedroom where her mother died, she thinks of the bullet hole in the wall that remained days later, while "everything seemed to carry the imprint of death."

And when you can remember only a few or no details, if you reveal your ignorance, loss of memory, and despair, the story you tell will include a depiction of the fragile dimensions of awareness.

Nothing has fortified my own memory so profoundly as gazing into courtyards, one of whose dark loggias, shaded by blinds in the summer, was for me the cradle in which the city laid its new citizen. The caryatids that supported the loggia on the floor above ours may have slipped away from their post for a moment to sing a lullaby beside that cradle—a song containing little of what later awaited me, but nonetheless sounding the theme through which the air of the courtyards has forever remained intoxicating to me.

—WALTER BENJAMIN,
Berlin Childhood Around 1900

Description

You are not expected to compile an exhaustive record of every detail regarding what you aim to describe. If your narrator happens to be an architect, then you may want to include the exact dimensions of the room she has just entered. Or if he is a clothing designer, he may tell you the length of the skirt that another character wears. In the first case, if your narrator is not an architect or builder, "small," "medium," "large," or "voluminous" will do, and in the second, unless we are listening to a designer, "long," "short," or "perilously short" will suffice. Regarding the skirt, its length will most probably carry meaning, reflecting either on the woman wearing it or on the man describing it.

Description often reveals as much about the observer as about the observed. However, the same rule applies to all descriptions: don't bore yourself. Describe what really interests or moves you (or would interest or move whoever is speaking in your story). In this way every description can play a double role, making us see things the way you or your character sees, while making the garden or lake or vase of flowers or neighborhood dogs come alive.

Whatever your subject is—be it a person, an event, or a concept—it did not appear from a vacuum. Everything and everyone arises from and is shaped by an environment. Regarding surroundings, whether it is the ball where Anna Karenina begins to fall in love with Vronsky, Mrs. Dalloway's London, or the courtyard in the building where Walter Benjamin lived as a child, the environment in which events take place is part of the story. And since an environment can rarely be disentangled from those who live within it, what is called "background" is usually ripe with significance. Understanding this turns description from a dull task into a meaningful exploration. What details indicate a deeper or larger meaning in the story you are telling?

Such details do not have to complete the image but instead point out a direction. The reader's imagination will supply what is missing in the picture.

The same is true for characters. If you spell out every physical attribute of your characters, your description will be as tiresome to read as it was to construct. Instead, if you include a few evocative details, the very erect posture of a military man, the stooped spine of a clerk, the sweet smile of a child, you will evoke far more than you could ever capture with an earnest but ultimately failing arsenal of details. As Peter Mendelsund writes in *What We See When We Read*, "narratives are made richer by omission."

Literary characters are physically vague—they have only a few features, and these features hardly seem to matter—or rather these features matter only in that they help to refine a character's meaning. Character description is a kind of circumscription. A character's features help to delineate their boundaries—but these features don't help us truly picture a person . . . it is precisely what the text does not elucidate that becomes an invitation to our imaginations.

—PETER MENDELSUND,
What We See When We Read

Atmosphere

The atmosphere surrounding and within a story, sometimes called a backdrop, can serve to generate the right mood in which to read or write an account of events. Whether the story is true or fictional, the setting may be anywhere and anything—sailing on an ocean, in a forest, on a hill overlooking a city, or at the edge of a village in the countryside, such as can be found in Carlo Levi's account of his years spent exiled in a village in Italy, *Christ Stopped at Eboli*:

> An animal-like enchantment lay over the deserted village . . . Roosters were crowing; their afternoon song had none of the shrillness of their early morning call, but reflected rather the bottomless sadness of the desolate countryside. The sky was filled with black crows and, above them, circling hawks; their still round eyes seemed to follow me.

The atmosphere can be established with a view, a scent, a covert glance, a photograph, a memory or a sound, even heard through closed windows, as in Curzio Malaparte's novel, *Kaputt*: "A sad yearning wail was swept with the wind . . ."

The setting might also be historical or conceptual, the tenor of the times, as with the famous opening lines of *A Tale of Two Cities*, by Charles Dickens:

> It was the best of times, it was the worst of times, it was the age of wisdom, it was the age of foolishness, it was the epoch of belief, it was the epoch of incredulity, it was the season of Light, it was the

season of Darkness, it was the spring of hope, it
was the winter of despair . . .

And while a setting often mirrors the mood of the narrator, it
can also intensify that mood by providing a stark contrast, as does
Marguerite Duras's description, in her memoir *The War*, of a sunny
day spent at the beach with her husband, soon after he returned
from a concentration camp.

But if the description of a setting can conjure the mood of a
scene to the reader, it can also reveal deeper sources of memory and
emotion to the writer. If you find yourself pausing and in need of
inspiration, try to describe the mood of your story or, alternatively,
your present setting and its atmosphere. What you consider mere
backdrop can be, on reflection, central to who you are and who you
will become, both on the page and in life.

Second Sight

Writing Is Rewriting

I learned early on that writing is rewriting.
—EMILY BERNARD IN CONVERSATION
WITH HONOR MOORE

One afternoon when I was watching my adoptive father as he brushed thick white paint over a figure he had painted the day before, he told me that he envied writers. "If you want to make changes you don't have to destroy the earlier version." Years later I was to remember these words when I read *A Giacometti Portrait*, as the author, James Lord, describes the months during which he sat for his friend, the great artist Giacometti, each morning returning to the artist's studio to discover with increasing dismay that the artist had destroyed all the work done the day before. Along with Lord, as I read, I shuddered at all that destruction. But the truth is that writing involves lots of destruction too. (Once I begin revising a sentence, I rarely revive its earlier incarnation.)

Now with computers (which only came into existence after I had already written several books), I delete and substitute several words before reaching the end of a sentence. But this does not prevent me from looking with a jaundiced eye in the morning at what I have done the day before, and rewriting it once or twice or three times again. This is called craft. And once you accept it as an inevitable part of the process, you will feel far more hopeful than you might have thought. Yes, yesterday afternoon, you believed that the paragraph you wrote was brilliant. But no, in the morning it just doesn't sound right. It's not nearly as good as you thought it was. But now you can begin in earnest to make the paragraph into what you mistakenly thought—or perhaps dreamed—that it was.

As far as I have been able to tell, what happens overnight is that you shift your perspective from the writer to the reader. The ideas and intentions for the pages you wrote the day before are no longer in the forefront of your mind, and so they no longer cloud your perception regarding what is actually on the page. Now a different task is before you. No longer generating ideas, instead you can focus on how to make your meaning clear to the reader. Or less awkward, or on good days, perhaps, even beautiful.

Though in actual practice the line between yourself as writer and yourself as reader is not as definitive as all that. Because as you correct, refine, and polish the words you wrote yesterday, new ideas will often come to mind. (So you find yourself reading and writing at the same time.)

With many writers the practice of correction becomes a habit, almost an addictive one. Several friends who write have told me that were it not impossible, they would go on correcting their work long after it was published. The pleasure of it is not unlike sanding a wooden table or chair or stitching a leather shoe, calmly practicing the art you've learned through reading and writing all of your life.

If you write with a pencil you get three different sights at it to see if the reader is getting what you want him to. First when you read it over; then when it is typed you get another chance to improve it, and again in the proof. Writing it first in pencil gives you one-third more chance to improve it. That is .333 which is a damn good average for a hitter. It also keeps it fluid longer so that you can better it easier.

—ERNEST HEMINGWAY,
By-Line: Ernest Hemingway

Well and Good

> . . . my rule has been, to write what I have to say
> the best way I can—then lay it aside—taking it up
> again after some time and reading it afresh—the
> mind new to it. If there's no jar in the new reading,
> well and good—that's sufficient for me.
>
> —WALT WHITMAN

When you are editing your own work, it is just as important to recognize what is good as it is to see what can and should be improved. (This is true even if you are editing someone else's work.) You can easily get into an industrious mode, measuring the worth of your labors by how much you change. Beware of this. When a scene or a sentence, paragraph, or passage is effective, moving, and/or beautiful (in other words when it is good), unless it undermines the whole work in some way, leave it alone. What makes for virtue in literature can be mysterious and, even if it seems powerful, delicate.

Despite the description of the way he worked that is quoted above, over many years, Walt Whitman published several different versions of his masterpiece, *Leaves of Grass*. Yet, despite all his efforts, or perhaps because of them, the second edition, published in 1856, is considered by many readers and critics as the best. Though there are some who prefer the 1860 edition and a few prefer the final edition, published in 1892, even if so many others believe he edited the life out of this version. I am grateful that the edition published in 1856 was preserved. (It is the one most often published today.)

In this light, keep your drafts at least for a year. When you look at your edits, a day or two or weeks or months later, you may want to reconsider the changes you've made. Above all, learn to value your own good work. And as part of this process, read aloud what you've written. Cadence is as vitally important as grammar; in fact, more so. If you don't understand this, choose any poem from *Leaves of Grass*, read it out loud, and you'll find out why sound is at the heart of the matter.

(How I Learned to Write)

I was fortunate in my teachers, one of whom taught a class in how to write creatively, and the other who taught his students how to write clearly.

Both classes explored the mysterious mechanics behind the miracles I had witnessed in literature. From the first I came away with an arsenal of craft, useful elements such as metaphor and foreshadowing. From the second teacher, I became aware of the structure of a sentence and how paragraphs and finally a whole essay (or even a book) can and should be shaped. In this way I learned how clarity, which in the end seems so simple, can be wrought out of the complexities of thought and language.

In the following years, while I earned a degree in English literature, I kept writing poetry, stories, essays, and movie reviews, publishing some, along with writing two plays (both produced to mixed reviews). But I had more to learn. And I was fortunate again to be given the opportunity, first as a proofreader and then a copy editor and finally a sometime staff writer for the progressive magazine *Ramparts*. By correcting and trying to improve what others had written, I learned how important it is to reread and edit my own work.

This was augmented by a perspective that I had begun to learn years earlier. After my adoptive father, Mort, had admired a series of short poems that I wrote while I was still in high school, I worked on them, trying to make them even better. But when I showed the new versions to Mort he was not pleased with what I had done. He felt, and he was right, that I had edited the life out of them. So early on I learned the caution that every editor needs to keep in mind in seeking improvement: as does a surgeon, one must be careful not to kill the patient.

Details

As you edit your work, pay attention to details. Think of a beautifully cut jacket that is missing two prominent buttons. Like an impeccable tailor, check everything as you edit your work, not just research but details like spelling or punctuation.

Years ago, my mentor and friend, Kay Boyle, taught me this. She corrected every small error in the manuscripts I showed her. When, as he emerged from his study, looking exhausted, Oscar Wilde, famous for his wit, was asked, "What did you do today?" he answered, "I spent all morning putting a comma in and all afternoon taking it out." That is of course exaggerated, but not by far. A misplaced comma can make a sentence incomprehensible.

Overwriting

Beware of overwriting. Like a nervous guest who smiles too much, it's a subtle effect but nevertheless erodes the trust of the reader. When a critic describes a passage in the book he is reviewing as *unfurling* a portrait of the city the author visited, your attention settles more on the word "unfurl" and less on what it aims to describe. Even if this is a creative use of language, the word is not quite right. Was the portrait done on a scroll? you find yourself asking, half unconsciously.

There's nothing intrinsically wrong with the verb "unfurl." Listen to how Ocean Vuong uses it in his remarkable novel, *On Earth We're Briefly Gorgeous*: "As Mrs. Callahan stood behind me, her mouth at my ear, I was pulled deeper into the current of language. The story unfurled, its storm rolled in as she spoke . . ." Surrounded as it is by the movements of a natural landscape, metaphorical storms and streams, the verb "unfurl" seems to belong here.

In the first example the word "unfurl" is vaguely confusing. In the second, because Vuong is aware of and extends the physical act of unfurling with the image of a storm, this word works to increase our understanding. When you aim at achieving clarity (which is called for not only to express ideas but to describe physical sensations and emotions too), other attributes, such as originality, will follow.

Redundancies and Tautologies

"But I don't want to go among mad people," Alice remarked.

"Oh, you can't help that," said the Cat: "we're all mad here. I'm mad. You're mad."

"How do you know I'm mad?" said Alice.

"You must be," said the Cat, "or you wouldn't have come here."

—LEWIS CARROLL, *Alice in Wonderland*

And here is a more recent and notable example of a tautology, from a member of former president Donald Trump's staff: "The President of the United States has the power of what the President of the United States has the power to do." Such circular logic often produces unintended humor, as this wonderful one from another politician: "If we do not succeed, we run the risk of failure."

Redundancies are not always tautologies; they do not argue so much as say the same thing twice, often boasting, as in "5G is a new innovation." Or they create the appearance that speakers do not understand the words they use, as in "The candidate tends to overexaggerate the crowds who come to his rallies," or the famous comment from Yogi Berra, "It's *deja vu* all over again." (*Deja vu* means "already seen.")

It's an easy mistake to make, to defend your argument simply by putting it into different words, or to emphasize a point by saying it twice. But in the end, tautologies and redundancies weaken prose as well as arguments. More importantly, they can truncate a train of thought. The impulse when you're not certain what to say next is to fall back on the tried and true—in other words to repeat yourself. If you do not prematurely close the process with repetition and instead allow yourself to be vulnerable, that is, not to know, or to be uncertain, you may well eventually discover new and perhaps greater insights.

Too Much or Too Little

There are two common habits that many writers share. One is to overwrite, too often boring readers or at least trying their patience. The other is to underwrite, saying too little, so that readers are confused and confounded or even disappointed.

Overwriting can be confused with abundance. But, paradoxically, too many words can impede the creative process. Instead of continuing on by telling us too much about something that is insignificant, you might have faced a pause in the development of your thought. And pauses, though they may at first feel uncomfortable, are full of potential meanings that have not yet come to the surface of consciousness. As with a silence in an intimate conversation, if you allow the pause to continue, sooner or later, you are more than likely to discover something you hadn't imagined was waiting to be said.

With underwriting, the idea or scene or character remains in a febrile state, undeveloped, unclear, and this too can impede the creative process. Being underdeveloped, what you have written is not ambulatory yet, so it cannot move forward.

Becoming aware of these habits is half the battle. And in both cases, it also helps to imagine a reader who, like a very good friend, grasps everything you say, who can even predict what you will say, but is still eager to hear you say it.

Regarding both habits, the underlying issue is usually trust.

PART III

The Means to an End

"Begin at the beginning," the King said, very gravely,
"and go on till you come to the end: then stop."

—LEWIS CARROLL,
Alice in Wonderland

Something

Now that you are approaching the end, you can see that you have created something. Whether it seems a predictable conclusion, a startling surprise, or it lands somewhere in between, the ending you write must feel as if it has grown naturally out of all that has come before. Otherwise, to the reader, it will feel contrived. As indeed it will be.

By This Time

Don't be afraid. Whether you know it or not, by this time, you've been creating lots of endings. You've ended a great number of sentences, of course, and though you may think that doesn't count, it does. You've had to assess the tensile strength of each sentence as you have built it. How much weight it was able to hold, or, speaking in more grammatical terms, how many verbs, clauses, adverbs, as well as ideas and actions and descriptions it could accommodate without collapsing under its own weight.

You must have ended countless paragraphs too. You had to hear the paragraph not once but at least twice, once as you wrote it and a second time as you read it back to yourself, and in this process rode the sound as if you were a surfer riding a wave to the shore, or a gymnast flying through the air, aiming to stick the landing. You may also have gauged the meaning and made minute decisions accordingly (and in concert with the sound of your words).

When I was a schoolgirl we were taught to begin a paragraph or an essay by introducing our subject, proceeding with arguments or descriptions, and ending with a conclusion that summarizes what was said. As dreary as this sounds, there is wisdom in it. The objective here is to consider the whole. How do the pieces fit together? Does the end reflect the beginning, in the way that the musical ending for an opera usually repeats themes heard in the overture? Or does the ending noticeably, even comically, or tragically, depart from the beginning, as in the bright young thing come to ruin?

If you're ending a book, you'll want to shift your focus from details to the sum of the parts. At which point in the narrative or argument or account do you wish to end? The answer is not always obvious. If you are writing an account of a wildfire in California, for instance, do you end when the fire has been put out? Or should you continue into the aftermath, following residents as they decide to leave or rebuild? Or do you continue by exploring the causes of the disaster, whether environmental, human, industrial, or all three?

The answer may be logical, reflecting your purpose as well as outcomes of the stories you've told. Or it may be aesthetic. Or both.

In any case, ask yourself what you have wrought. This moment, like all moments in the process of writing, is improvisational. What is the mood of the work as it stands? Where does this mood take you? With a sense of all you have done in mind, feel your way to the most beautiful, moving, or powerful end that is ready and waiting within the work.

Tying It All Up

It's not just the main plot. Of course, you'll need to solve the crime, or picture Elizabeth finally accepting Darcy's proposal, or depict Frederic as he watches Catherine die from childbirth, or let Gretta finally tell Gabriel what has been making her seem so distant. But you'll need to address all the other subplots and concerns, if not at the end, along the way to the end. In fact, addressing these issues can prepare the way for an ending, not only in the reader's mind but in your own, as you write.

Subplots do not need to be solved so much as confronted. Think of the retreat of the Italian army that Hemingway describes so brilliantly in *A Farewell to Arms*. A mood of disillusion, defeat, and shame slowly builds as Frederic shoots one of his men for refusing an order and then narrowly escapes execution by the military police himself, for retreating. Catherine's death mirrors and continues a mood of desolation and shame that ebbs and flows, reflected even by the weather, which provides one more subplot. If the night is clear and beautiful, as after Catherine's labor begins, she and Frederic make their way to the hospital, and when the birth begins to prove difficult, it starts to rain. Hemingway does not have to tell us that Frederic feels empty or purposeless or lost when Catherine dies. He's done that already by addressing all the elements of the story. His spare and blunt prose more than suffices at the end: "After a while I went out and left the hospital and walked back to the hotel in the rain."

On the eve of the first day, I know what will happen in the first chapter. Then, day after day, chapter after chapter, I find what comes later.

—GEORGES SIMENON

Irresolution

Some dilemmas and mysteries are not meant to be solved by the writer, or cannot be, in which case the best course is to admit the failure, as does Elizabeth Hardwick in her short biography of Melville, in which she admits at the end of a chapter, "so much about Melville is *seems to be*, *may have been*, and *perhaps*."

Finished but Not Ended

How is this possible? You've finished the book but it hasn't ended. Yet. The answer lies in the prose, the words, the book itself, not in the tale you're telling. Say you are writing a short biography of Proust as Edmund White has done in *Marcel Proust*. The story is finished on page 138 when White tells us that on November 18, 1922, Marcel drew his last breath and four days later was buried at Père Lachaise.

But the book ends on page 140.

In the two pages between finishing the story and ending his book, White ruminates briefly on the meaning of Proust's work, especially to readers today, who look at the Belle Époque, the era he portrayed so well, less as reality than fable. But mainly, White tells us, the work survives because of how it describes the rise and fall of both love and "grand social classes." Then White delivers his coup de grâce, which is the ending of his book. "Proust," he writes, "is the first contemporary writer of the twentieth century, for he was the first to describe the permanent instability of our times."

White could have ended with a sad burial, or with an anxious vigil at Marcel's bedside; either scene would have been moving. But the ending he has given us is far more appropriate to what he has written in the previous 138 pages. Because *Marcel Proust* is a book as much about literature as it is about a life, and as such is full of questions and insights about the choices Proust made as a writer.

White's last line has another virtue. In its piercing perception, both about Proust's work and the twentieth century, it functions as a framing line. For just as the frame around a window has both a top and a bottom, writing can and should be framed both at the beginning and the end. If your experience of a work is framed by the opening lines, the way you remember it will be framed by the ending and, in your memory, will color all that has come before.

The master of endings that not only frame but deepen your understanding of the narrative you have just read is Henry James. For an example, read *The Wings of the Dove*. Don't read the last line until you reach the end. Doing so would ruin the effect, one that you have to experience to understand. It's an effect any writer would want to create. But sad to say I cannot (nor, I believe, can anyone else) tell you how to do it. Until the code is cracked, we'll have to classify it as a miracle.

Closing the Circle

Inanna crowned herself!

—KIM ECHLIN, *Inanna: From the*
Myths of Ancient Sumer

This is simple advice, a practice that most writers have used more than once. When you have finished telling (or reporting) a story, or elucidating your argument, and tied up all the loose ends (if not solving every dilemma, at least acknowledging that you were unable to do so)—in short, if you have finished, then one of the first places to search for an ending is to look toward the beginning.

Over millennia, perhaps even before the written word, folk and traditional forms have used a line that occurs near the beginning, and repeats more than once through the telling, to end a work. So a Scottish Gaelic folk prayer begins "Greetings to you, gem of the night" and ends "Majesty of the stars, gem of the night!" Or a Serbo-Croatian song, which begins "O, my hero. *Đerđelez Alija!* Send the wedding guests whenever you wish," ends with the same invitation, "Send the wedding guests whenever you wish."

This practice has stayed with us across many cultures for centuries. Federico García Lorca, who was deeply influenced by the Spanish folk poems, called "Deep Songs," used it, as in his *Casida del Llanto*, in which the last line of the first stanza is "nothing else is heard but the weeping," which is also the last line of the poem. Dylan Thomas uses a similar pattern in "Do Not Go Gentle into That Good Night," the first stanza of which contains the lines, "Old age should burn and rave at close of day;/Rage, rage against the dying of the light," and ends by repeating the line "Rage, rage against the dying of the light." And of course there is Leonard

Cohen's song "Hey, That's No Way to Say Goodbye," the title of which repeats throughout and ends the song.

Such returns inscribe a circle, one of the fundamental forms of human existence. We live on a sphere that turns and over a year circles another sphere, a circle we are relieved to see rise most mornings. Another circle rises at night. And we are all on a circular journey as we age. *From dust thou art and to dust thou shall return.* The food that nurtures us is tied to the seasons or cycles of nature, and we also rely on family circles and circles of friends for sustenance.

If weaving a thread from the beginning to the end of a work gives it an almost indefinable, tensile strength, one that is deeply satisfying, even when the tale being told does not end happily, paradoxically, repetition can also act as a measure of change. When a line is repeated at the end of a stanza or verse, the meaning of that line has often garnered at least one other dimension of meaning.

To close the circle, you can recognize what has occurred as a form of karma, causation, or logic. Or the circle can be closed with a statement that justice, rhyme, or reason are all absent. All of the above can be implied instead of stated. Your ending may not reflect the beginning in any way you can recognize. But in any case, to find the right ending, it will help you to look again at the beginning, ponder what you have wrought, and then summon the powers that have driven your work to introduce the silence to ensue.

Casida of Crying

I have shut the balcony
so I will not hear those cries,
but behind these grey walls
there is nothing but crying.
So few angels are singing
so few dogs even bark;
a thousand violins fit
in the palm of my hand.
But the crying is an immense dog
the crying is an immense angel
the crying is an immense violin
and as tears quiet the wind,
there is nothing to hear but crying.

—FEDERICO GARCÍA LORCA

(TRANS. SUSAN GRIFFIN)

Starting with the End

At times the ending of a work will come to you as you are writing your first pages (or even before). Then your task is to earn whatever ending you have conceived early in the process of writing. In such cases, your ending often serves as both a template and a goal, giving you the emotional tone of the journey as well as the destination, affecting everything you write, casting a light here and a shadow there, shaped by what lies ahead.

If I didn't know the ending of a story, I wouldn't begin. I always write my last lines, my last paragraph, my last page first, and then I go back and work towards it.

—KATHERINE ANN PORTER, QUOTED IN
JILL KREMENTZ, *The Writer's Desk*

Where It Is, It Ain't

Ida Rolf, the woman who created the famous method of healing known as "Rolfing," was famous for saying, "Where it is, it ain't." What she wanted her students to understand is that when a patient suffers pain or other problems in one part of the body, such as slumped shoulders, the solution often lies elsewhere, for instance in the muscles around the torso. In this way she was engaging in what is called "systems thinking," as she looked at her patients with the understanding that in the body, everything is connected.

This is true of literature too, in every form. What you write on page one will still be casting its influence on page 1005. Keeping this in mind, when you are having trouble finishing, look toward the beginning to see if, to use another metaphor, you made a wrong turn somewhere on your journey. When you've made a wrong turn, the directions you've been following will no longer make any sense. Perhaps you've killed off a character who needs to be alive to give the evidence that is crucial in solving the crime. Or, in an essay, perhaps you've introduced two issues, but then addressed only one.

In your search for the problem, listen closely to your own complaints. Every writer has to learn to distinguish between a visionary like Cassandra and an anxiety-filled alarmist, both of whom live inside most of us.

Deus ex Machina

You can, if you want, vanquish your antagonists and save your protagonists at the very end with the spectacular arrival of Superwoman (or man). You would not be the first to employ such a device. It's been used in a great many very successful narratives, whether films or comic books or even novels. But to be believable, such heroics should not be sprung on the reader as if out of thin air at the last moment.

This kind of dubious practice has a name. It is called *deus ex machina*. The term comes from a technique developed for popular Greek and Roman theater, and later those improvised plays with stock characters known as commedia dell'arte, performed by the Italian troupes who traveled from town to town throughout Europe during the late Renaissance. Whenever the actors got their heroes and/or heroines in a seemingly unsolvable quandary, they could alter fate by using a crane to lower a god or an angel over the stage, a figure that of course would resolve every conflict in favor of the just and the righteous.

The problem with such an ending is not that it involves supernatural powers. Where would we be in fiction and fantasy without that shining element? No. The problem is that it's hard to believe anything, be it force or person, that is introduced at the end. In such cases, as readers, we are bound to feel manipulated or cheated or both. If you want Superman (or woman) to appear at the end you've got to introduce this figure far earlier in your story. (For instance, show Clark Kent donning his cape.) And you might also consider introducing some impediments your superhero faces in attempting a rescue. In other words, in order to believe your ending, even if it is a surprise, your reader must feel that it was there developing its potential, even out of sight, throughout most of the story, so that it arrives organically, even if unpredicted.

This principle applies to many different plots as well as to nonfiction. For instance, in a novel, speaking generally, you don't want a new character to appear in the last chapter (unless of course this character has been referred to and talked about and missed or feared by others characters, even if absent). The same goes for your character's feelings, which may be revealed at the end if, as with Elizabeth's attraction to Darcy, you suspected they were there all the time under the surface. Regarding nonfiction, when you are discussing an unfortunate decision made by the president of the United States, you don't want to chalk it all up to his childhood in the last paragraphs. The subject of his childhood should be introduced earlier and developed in various ways, subtle or not, throughout.

But in all cases, as with any weaving, all the threads must be introduced in the beginning, accounted for, pulled through, and tied at the end to prevent the fabric from unraveling. And perhaps this too is a mirror of justice.

Hecuba: Zeus, whether you are the necessity of nature or the mind of mortal men, I address you in prayer! For proceeding on a silent path, you direct all mortal affairs toward justice!

—EURIPIDES, *The Trojan Women*
(TRANS. DAVID KOVACS)

The Moral of the Story

One of the oldest ways to end a tale is with a lesson. This was a common practice well before the sixth century B.C.E., when a man held in bondage, called Aesop, told his tales. Aesop's fables are still with us, the animals in his imagination still showing us how we ought and ought not to behave.

The practice was still prevalent in the fourteenth century, during the time of Chaucer. Many of his *Canterbury Tales* end with a moral, often religious, as in "The Physician's Tale": "Give up sin or sin will leave you dying."

Malcolm X ends his autobiography with a prayer that is in its own way a moral lesson: "And if I can die having brought any light, having exposed any meaningful truth that will help to destroy the racist cancer that is malignant in the body of America—then, all of the credit is due to Allah. Only the mistakes have been mine."

Hannah Arendt ends her account of the trial of Adolf Eichmann, a man responsible for the mass murder of millions, with this thought: "It was as though in those last minutes, he was summing up the lesson that this long course in human wickedness had taught us—the lesson of the fearsome, word-and-thought-defying *banality of evil*."

In the examples above, the moral seems to spring organically from what has gone before. These conclusions enlarge the meaning of what has gone before, not just conceptually, but emotionally too.

Peroration

Whether the ending of a speech or an essay, a peroration sums up what has been said or written with words that call up strong emotion. Perorations have a bad reputation because they are so often used by various scoundrels who appeal to base feelings, as they try to whip up their followers to dubious ends. Yet, not only do perorations provide strong and memorable endings, they have a way of bringing us together too. Think of Dr. Martin Luther King Jr.'s famous speech, ending with a list of promises, each beginning with the phrase "I have a dream." With this moving peroration, he forged a community out of a vision of a just world.

Ambiguity

Literature can mirror life in countless ways, including both the capacity of the human mind to reach clear conclusions and the failure in many cases to do so. Is it really clear that the designated villain committed the crime in question? In life this poses a very difficult if not dangerous problem. But in literature, you can create a stunning conclusion from the lack of clarity. Maybe she did the deed and maybe not. Maybe the couple you portrayed saved their marriage, but perhaps they did not. Maybe once he's inherited a million dollars, Jack will finally be happy. But . . . given his character, perhaps not.

The best conclusion is always the one that is true, even if the truth is that you don't know. And for this you need logic, of course, but you will also need to listen to your own work. The sound of your prose will take you into the intuitive realm of consciousness from which the work was created. The French writer Patrick Modiano is a master of ambiguity. He ends his novella *Afterimage* by telling us that the central character, whom the narrator has sought, and whose whereabouts he has puzzled over, has dropped out of sight. Before he disappeared, this man told the narrator that he no longer knew who he was. This is an ending that paradoxically contains more knowledge than a simple solution to the puzzle would.

While you are aiming at the future, searching for a conclusion that does not exist yet, ask yourself if what you dismissed as an impediment to your final vision is in fact the solution you've been seeking. That is—you don't know—and that too is part of the human condition, one that, indeed, once you accept it, can be deeply satisfying to portray.

Ending with an Image

This is the way Oliver Sacks ends the chapter in his *Oaxaca Journal* that he calls "Thursday." He focuses on the vegetation in the valley through which he has traveled, weaving this subject with the story of the Spanish invasion and their oppression of the people indigenous to the valley. Braiding the two subjects together, he discusses the deep red color treasured by the Spanish and worn by their soldiers in their unforms. The source of the dye is the cochineal, an insect that lives on prickly pear cactus. So it seems organic, entirely natural, when he ends this chapter by telling us, "I make a blood red smear of cochineal in my notebook . . ." invoking both the cactus and the terrible slaughter endured by the Indians in one stroke.

It is a stunning image, one hard to forget, which is exactly what you wish for in an ending.

Ending with a Metaphor

In her wondrously structured essay "Peonies," Zadie Smith begins by picturing herself, along with two other middle-aged women, peering into the Jefferson Market Garden in New York. She was expecting peonies and for this reason she is disappointed to find, instead, tulips. Noting (in ten short pages) that she is aware of the Freudian implications of women her age, near menopause, "drawn to a gaudy symbol of fertility," she rides a stream of thought about women, creation, change, death, and the nature of consciousness, while quoting Nabokov and Kierkegaard in the process before landing in a bed of flowers again: "And once in a while a vulgar strain of spring flower will circumvent a long trained and self-consciously downtown aesthetic."

What seems relevant and even crucial to add here is that metaphors are not always, nor even often, conjured from thin air but can survive outside of consciousness too, even if eventually they carry us beyond the physical boundaries of space and time.

The seventh reader interrupts you: "Do you believe that every story must have a beginning and an end? In ancient times a story could end only in two ways: having passed all the tests, the hero and heroine married, or they died. The ultimate meaning to which all stories refer has two faces: the continuity of life, the inevitability of death."

You stop for a moment to reflect on these words. Then, in a flash, you decide you want to marry Ludmilla.

—ITALO CALVINO,
If on a Winter's Night a Traveler

A Reversal of Fortune

It's an expected surprise in mystery stories. Agatha Christie does it often. The one who seemed suspiciously avaricious or evasive turns out to be reliable and decent. The one who seemed above reproach—yes, that nice-looking, easygoing chap—turns out to be the real villain. Reversals often occur before the actual last words in the story and even before all the plot elements are resolved. I am thinking of *Les Misérables* and the moment when Javert, the policemen who has been relentlessly pursuing the hero, Valjean, commits suicide. This is a major resolution of a harrowing narrative, but not the end of the story. Yet it seems right that this should occur near and not at the end, allowing the final ending to occur in a relatively serene and reflective mood.

It is not always necessary to finish the villain off. Sherlock Holmes's nemesis, the evil Moriarty, disappears instead of perishing, giving his creator, Arthur Conan Doyle, the option of future struggles in books to come. But in his stories there is usually another plot, the mystery the detective is aiming to solve, and that almost always involves a reversal, if not of fate, then of judgment.

In great works, like *King Lear*, both fate and judgment are changed as when Lear confronts the terrible consequences of his narcissism.

A reversal is a very satisfying way to end a work. Perhaps this is because while riveted and then satisfied, we are also edified, and in this way we learn to remain fluid in the way we think.

The Ineffable

There are phenomena which the wiser among us understand would be easily crushed by definition. You had to be there, as is said, or have felt it, or you will know it when you see it. So in his essay "Theory and Play of the Duende," Federico García Lorca, never tells us what "duende" is. And at the end, after asking, "Where is the duende?" he gives us his beautiful and thoroughly elusive answer: "Through the empty arch comes a wind, a mental wind blowing relentlessly over the heads of the dead, in search of new landscapes and unknown accents; a wind that smells of baby's spittle, crushed grass and jellyfish veil, announcing the constant baptism of newly created things."

When the question you have posed has an answer that cannot be put into words, or an answer that is still a secret no one is willing to tell you yet, your ending can be provided by the problem itself, by admitting that you don't know how to describe answer, or can't reveal it, or, as in Lorca's case, when the answer cannot be reduced to words. Don't try to cover up the vacuum. Even in absence, the truth is always interesting.

Echoes

When you reach the end, you may have created a running theme or a narrative that you did not anticipate in the beginning. This is when you should go back and find a place earlier in the work where, knowing what you do now, you can insert a few words or a passage that prepares the way for what's to come with whatever is called for—a hint, a suggestion, an image, another element of the narrative, such as a dream or even a minor character. Above all avoid piling up any or all of this at the end. This would only create clutter if not a ragged edge, and, more important, disbelief.

At the suggestion of my editor, after I finished writing and subsequently settled on a title for a book called *A Chorus of Stones*, I added a brief passage to the first chapter that made a reference to the stones that wept when Orpheus sang. In that way, instead of intruding on the end, in which a young painter gazes into the rocks that line her route of escape from fascist soldiers, those weeping stones could still be heard as an echo resonating throughout the book.

... perhaps we are like stones; our own history and the history of the world embedded in us, we hold a sorrow deep within and cannot weep until that history is sung.

—SUSAN GRIFFIN, *A Chorus of Stones*

Ambivalence

Despite long weeks, months, and even years of anticipating the completion of your work, as you near the finish line, it is not at all uncommon to feel ambivalent. After all, this work has occupied your mind daily, even on days when you spent no time writing; as you engaged in a long conversation full of meaning, beauty, and moments of humor if not sorrow and grief, it has been your constant companion. Added to which you may feel a fear, common to many writers, that the work will be rejected by the outside world.

Paradoxically, you may at the same time be tugged in the opposite direction, toward haste. Thus you can find yourself rushing toward the end, hoping to put the whole project out of its misery.

In this way you may encounter still another emotional challenge, one that, despite the clamor of fear and regret, requires you to invoke an inner stillness and focus. The way you end a work is as important as the way you begin it. Breathe. Focus. Take your time, yet try not to avoid the inevitable.

Stragglers

Of course, you could go on infinitely adding aspects or scenes or moments or insights. Others to whom you may show your manuscript, or portions of it, will have suggestions too. Some of these ideas may even be reasonable. "Really if you're writing about romance in the fifties, you must include Doris Day and Rock Hudson," a friend might say. If you must add these two, go ahead, but not at the end, unless you want your ending to feel like my garage looks, with odds and ends and no integrity of form at all.

(How I Learned to Write)

One summer, after I turned twenty, I moved to North Beach where I shared an apartment with two other women in a gray stucco building at the top of Grant Avenue. Because I wanted to write plays, I began to study improvisational acting at The Committee, a theater, just down the hill on Broadway. In a sense, I devoted the whole summer to improvisation, since at night my friends and I, carrying the discarded identity papers of older friends of friends, would go to hear the jazz that was performed nightly on the other end of Broadway. In the bargain, I learned far more about writing than I anticipated I would. As I took in the exquisite but unpredictable music of John Coltrane, Ornette Coleman, Carmen McRae, and heeded the instructions in my acting class to stay in the moment, observe what is present, be aware of my impulses and run with them, I began to realize that every creation holds stunning surprises, a unique beauty, present all the time, all the way through to the end.

Ending with Ceremony

A brief one, of course. Usually consisting of a single ceremonial sentence or phrase, for instance, "And they lived happily ever after." Or a direct signal to the audience, as in "My story now is done," "And here it ends," or "My tale is told." Or a ceremonial nod to the future, as with "As far as I know, they are still living there today." Or, if another subject should arise, "But that is another story." Or the affirmative, "And so it was." And there is always the very brief "Amen."

The ceremonial ending might also include a direct address or salutation to the reader, as in the challenge expressed in the ending of an Italian folktale, collected and retold by Italo Calvino: "So goes my little tale/Now it is your turn/All of us to regale."

And here at the end of this book that you hold in your hands I shall give you one more example of an ending with a salutation:

I salute you, dear writer, and wish you well as you bring sound out of silence and create something, where before you believed there was nothing.

Acknowledgments

Let me first thank my many teachers, including Josephine Miles, Tillie Olsen, and the late, extraordinary Kay Boyle, and my many students, some of whom offered support of various kinds, recently Marian Burke, Rebecca Foust, Ann Foley, Olivia Sears, and Elizabeth Gould, who, along with Anthony Rio, very kindly, during the pandemic, brought me groceries and sometimes flowers. Justine Shapiro read early chapters and also brought groceries. I owe much gratitude to Elizabeth Rosner, who read a draft and offered her fine and perceptive editorial suggestions. Nina Wise read early drafts of several chapters and was encouraging and insightful, as was Cherilyn Parsons, Anita Barrows, Nancy Shelby, and Deborah Dallinger, who, along with her wife, Jodi Rose, also did some shopping for me.

I want to thank Jack Shoemaker for early comments, my editor Jennifer Alton for her sparing but very useful suggestions, the fine production editor Laura Berry, and my supportive and empathetic agent, Andy Ross.

I would also like to take this occasion to thank all those members of my community who helped me survive in these times with their support both emotional and material. I am especially grateful to Susanna Dakin for her very kind generosity. And to Alice Walker for whose support and kindness I am very grateful. Thanks also for their generosity to Mary and Steve Swig, the late Bokara Legendre, Sylvia Brownrigg, Donna Brookman, Kaaren Kitchell, Leonard Pitt, Darren Aronofsky, Jim Hodges, John Harris, Deirdre English and Wayne Herkness, Arlie and Adam Hochschild, Marty Krasney, Jodie Evans, Donna Deitch and Terri Jentz, Kirsten Grimstad and Diana Gould for their steadfast kindness, David Shaddock, Mike Klein and Nancy Duff for their efforts in keeping me sheltered, old friends, Ken Cloke, Jeanne Varon, and Mike Miller, Lyn Hejinian and Poets in Need for their aid. Thanks to Lee Swenson and Vijaya Nagarajan for providing a platform for my support, Claire Greensfelder, Kathleen McLean, and Belvie Rooks for wise practical advice and abiding friendship. Let me also thank the artful and skillful Joan Miura who helped to prepare my archives for the Schlesinger Library at Radcliffe, Harvard. And to all those, too numerous to mention, who also contributed to my well-being in this period in countless ways, I am deeply grateful.

© Irene Young

SUSAN GRIFFIN has written more than twenty-two books, including nonfiction, poetry, and plays. *A Chorus of Stones: The Private Life of War* was a finalist for the Pulitzer Prize and a *New York Times* Notable book. *Woman and Nature*, considered a classic of environmental writing, is credited for inspiring the ecofeminist movement. She and her work have been awarded a Guggenheim Fellowship, an Emmy, and the Fred Cody Award for Lifetime Achievement & Service, among other honors. She lives in the San Francisco Bay Area. Find out more at susangriffin.com.